A Corner in the Marais

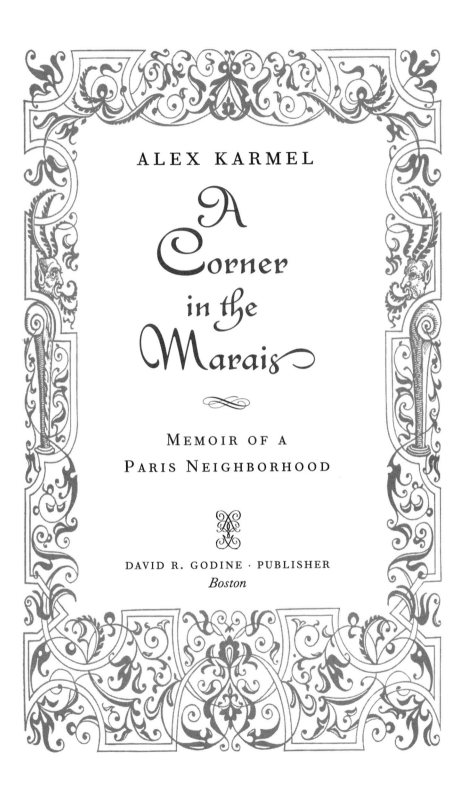

ALEX KARMEL

A Corner in the Marais

MEMOIR OF A
PARIS NEIGHBORHOOD

DAVID R. GODINE · PUBLISHER
Boston

First published in 1998 by
David R. Godine, Publisher, Inc.
Box 450
Jaffrey, New Hampshire 03452

*I would like to thank Mme. Michèle Debaecker for her help in transcribing documents from the
Archives de l'Assistance Publique.—AK*

Lines from "The Last Time I Saw Paris" by Jerome Kern and Oscar Hammerstein II, reprint-
ed by permission of PolyGram Music Publishing. Copyright © 1940 PolyGram International
Publishing, Inc. Copyright renewed. All rights reserved.
Excerpt from *Le Piéton de Paris* by Léon-Paul Fargue reprinted by arrangement with
Editions Gallimard, Paris. Copyright © 1939 by Editions Gallimard.

ILLUSTRATIONS CREDITS:
Alex Karmel: 16, 33, 34, 48, 57, 65, 98, 102, 110, 113, 116, 124, 137;
James P. Blair: 20, 21, 29, 58, 60, 97, 127, 132, 134, 139;
Musée Carnavalet/Photothèque des Musées de la Ville de Paris: 53, 54, 62, 79, 143;
Keystone Photo: 24, 26, 105; Caisse des Monuments Historiques (Paris): 36, 101, 129;
Musée du Louvre: 84; Bibliothèque Nationale: 131;
Pascal Servouze: 142; Michel Baret/Rapho: 145.

Library of Congress Cataloging in Publication Data
Karmel, Alex, 1931-
A corner in the Marais: memoir of a Paris neighborhood / Alex Karmel.
p.   cm.
1. Karmel, Alex, 1931-   —Homes and haunts—France—Marais (Paris)
2. Marais (Paris, France)—History. I. Title.
DC752.M37K37   1997
944'.36—DC20   96-33093 CIP

ISBN: 1-56792-074-8

Second printing, 1998

Contents

For my wife,
Marianne

Foreword

THIS IS NOT a guidebook to the neighborhood known as the Marais, although it might serve to open the eyes of the casual stroller to what he comes upon in its byways. Nor does it pretend to be a complete history of the place, though there is certainly much of that. The point of view is personal, and so it begins with my own discovery of Paris. Among the great world cities, Paris has the distinction of conveying its essence immediately to anyone who arrives with an open mind. My approach, then, has been not so much that of an historian as of a memoirist, if we accept the dictionary definition of *memoir* as "a record of events, of history treating of matters from the personal knowledge of the writer or with reference to particular sources of information" (*Oxford English Dictionary*).

The "particular sources of information" here are not only the documents on which the third chapter, "An Auction," are based (so far as I know, this is the first time they have been investigated), but also, in a larger sense, my own experience of having lived in the Marais for nearly fifteen years, as well as my individual interpretation of what might be considered general knowledge. As an American, I have always seen things through American eyes—which might explain, for example, the pages devoted to Beaumarchais's activities as a gun-runner during the American War of Independence, neither the best-known nor the most important episode in his tumultuous life.

Finally, there is the particular information that comes from personal context. I have centered this memoir on a specific building in the Marais, and built the history of the neighborhood (and to some extent, the city) from the standpoint of that one spot. The building has no special distinction apart from the fact that it has been standing for centuries, and that some years ago my wife and I purchased a small apartment just under its roof (that purchase, too, forms part of the story). In other words, though this building has "witnessed" many events and upheavals, it has been directly involved in few of them—and so much the better. Indeed, what has always interested me most in history is not the lives of great men or the analysis of the social, political, and economic forces that determined the great events, but rather the attempt to recreate a sense of what it was like to be an ordinary person living in a given era. For all the fascinating studies of the "mentalities" of different periods, I believe there is a common humanity on which we can rely in interpreting the past.

The Marais, however, is not merely the past; it is also a vibrant, living neighborhood in the present. And it is this sense of overlapping continuity and evolution that I have most wanted to convey in the pages that follow, as I (and many others before me) have observed them from my ordinary corner.

—ALEX KARMEL

Paris, 1997

A Corner in the Marais

"The Last Time I Saw Paris"

MY FIRST VIEW OF PARIS was of the backs of the apartment houses that overlook the tracks leading to the Gare du Nord. It was a cool, grey morning in June 1949; I was not quite eighteen. I was traveling with André, a Swiss friend who, like me, had just completed his freshman year at Columbia. We had crossed the Atlantic on a small Dutch freighter that had a cut-rate dormitory for students: twelve days of rainy weather from Hoboken to Antwerp at the speed of a leisurely bicycle rider. It was my first trip to Europe. Our plans for the summer were the Grand Tour on a very small budget.

During the train ride from Brussels, a woman in our compartment had strongly recommended a small hotel on rue de Bassano, not far from the Etoile. We took her advice: the place was, as promised, clean and reasonable. At lunch we noticed that the clientele was mainly comprised of long-faced South Americans, who filled the cream-painted dining room with a sedate babble of Spanish. The food, however, was French, though very plain French, characterized by the coarse texture of the puree of watercress soup which André and I would discover was served at almost every meal.

Three exhausting days later, during which we learned a lot about the metro and bus lines, André was suddenly stricken with nausea, cramps, and fever: all the symptoms of appendicitis. André's parents were in Cannes, but we couldn't immediately get in touch with them. I asked the hotel to get us a doctor, and I also called an aunt and uncle of mine who happened to be traveling through Paris just then. My aunt and the doctor arrived at the same time.

It soon became clear that an operation was imperative; the doctor had already made arrangements for André to be admitted to a "clinic" not far away, on rue du Dôme, a converted Second Empire town house with a bronze plaque saying that Baudelaire had died there. In short order I saw my friend being wheeled into the operating room; fortunately, he fared better than Baudelaire.

Later I got through to Cannes, and that night André's mother took the *Train Bleu* to Paris. In the morning she went straight to the clinic to make sure André was all right, then took me to lunch at Prunier's, my first really good French meal. The rest of André's family and entourage arrived over the next two days (the last being the chauffeur driving the white Cadillac) and moved into the four-star Hotel Napoléon on the other side of the Champs-Elysées. I remained in the hotel on rue de Bassano, listening to the discreet Spanish buzzing as I sipped my watercress soup.

We had been planning to spend only ten days in Paris before heading south toward Italy; now everything had to be changed. André was kept in the clinic for a week, that being the way it was done in those days; then he moved into the Hotel Napoléon with his family. Every morning I went to see André, sometimes participating in family discussions that often resembled disputes. But most of the time I was on my own, alone in a big city where I didn't know anyone and with only a limited command of the language. And yet, during those three or four weeks I was completely happy, vibrantly happy, as one is at the start of a love affair.

I don't quite remember what I did with my time. The weather was wonderful and I walked a great deal. I went to the Arc de Triomphe and the Eiffel Tower; I visited Notre Dame and the Louvre, where many of the paintings shocked me by their billboard size. I went to Montmartre in search of Utrillo and to Montparnasse in search of Hemingway and to Saint-Germain-des-Prés in search of "Existentialists." My daily indulgence was a *citron pressé* (lemonade) at Fouquet's on the Champs-Elysées while I read what I could of the *Figaro*, which was mainly the advertisements.

But for the most part I was simply happy to be in Paris, which that summer meant above all the Paris of Haussmann, the long straight boulevards with their chestnut trees, wide sidewalks, and welcoming café terraces. The only place where I talked to anyone aside from André and his family was in the line of tourists waiting to change travelers' checks at the American Express bureau on rue Scribe. I remember one woman who said she didn't understand why people made such a fuss about Paris: aside from Montmartre, which was "cute," it was just another Washington, DC, with more traffic. I thought she was demented. I never even wondered why I was so happy during those three weeks, just walking around alone, but then when you are seventeen happiness is not a state that you question; it seems perfectly normal.

After André was deemed well enough to leave Paris, we all went back to his home town of Geneva, where he and I spent ten relatively dull days on the shores of Lake Leman. After that we left by bus for the Riviera and Italy, finally returning to Paris in the last days of August, just before our Dutch freighter was to leave for the United States. It was then that I discovered for the first time the pleasure of coming *back* to Paris; back to what had become the place in which I was most happy, despite all the fascination of Rome and Florence. It was then also that I first had the feeling that coming back to Paris was coming home, and that leaving it—for what was, after all, my real home—was leaving something of myself behind as well.

☙ ☙ ☙

It was only sixteen years later that I began to question my adolescent joy. My wife, Marjorie, had died, and I was in analysis trying to make sense of my life. Psychoanalysis, at its best, can be something like a detective story where you suddenly remember all the hidden clues that have been there all along in the first chapters of the book. In my case the solution to this particular mystery all began with a short film called, inevitably, *The Last Time I Saw Paris*.

That, of course, is the name of a charming book by the American journalist Elliot Paul, who had lived in Paris in the thirties and described his life there once back in America—a wistful story made all the more poignant by the fact that when it was published, Paris was occupied by the Germans. Elliot Paul had lived on the Left Bank near Notre Dame, on rue de la Huchette, a street that is now in the pedestrian zone behind Saint-Séverin Church. In its present avatar, rue de la Huchette could not be less typical of traditional Paris, being almost entirely lined with Greek and North African restaurants. It is also the home of the tiny Théâtre de la Huchette, where Ionesco's first two plays, *The Lesson* and *The Bald Soprano,* have been playing without interruption for forty years.

Be that as it may, the title of Paul's memoir was so good that someone made it into a sentimental song that became a hit during the war:

> *The last time I saw Paris,*
> *Her heart was warm and gay—*
> *No matter how they change her,*
> *I'll remember her that way...*

And then someone made a short anti-Nazi film with the song as the sound track, a sort of forties MTV. It had clips of pigeons on the square in front of Notre Dame and young couples kissing on the quays and the traffic circling the Arc de Triomphe. And then there were shots of German battalions goose-stepping down the Champs-Elysées and Hitler dancing a jig on the terrace at Trocadéro.

I saw *The Last Time I Saw Paris* when I was eleven, at a time when my mother was dying of cancer. What came out in my analysis was that in watching this rather sentimental short film, I seem to have identified the city of Paris, ravaged by the Nazis, with my mother, ravaged by the disease that killed her. So that finding myself actually in Paris some years later was like a resurrection, a miracle.

It seems to me, though, that I was trying to find an explanation for something which to most people seems perfectly normal. Falling in love with Paris is not usually considered a pathological symptom. When I returned to New York, no one had been surprised that I had found Paris the high point of my trip. And three years later, when I was taking my Master's degree, my advisor found it perfectly normal that my choice of courses should be strongly influenced by my desire to return to the French capital. Indeed, the two of us concocted a research project for my application for a Fulbright scholarship that could be done only in Paris, and the proposal was accepted.

It never even entered my head that I might not find Paris as totally enchanting four years later as it had been on my first visit. As it happened, I found it all I remembered and more. Arriving in June, I stayed for two weeks in a small hotel on rue des Ecoles, most of which time I again spent wandering around alone. Then I left regretfully to meet up with some friends in Spain, where I was joined by my girlfriend from New York. By the time the summer was over, Marjorie and I were engaged. When she went back to New York, I was lucky enough to find an affordable room just under the eaves of a small hotel on the Ile Saint-Louis. No view of the Seine, except when you stood looking out the narrow gabled window in the bathroom.

The Ile Saint-Louis was already a favorite spot for foreigners in Paris, especially Americans, but not yet as tourist-ridden as it has become today. Marjorie came back from New York in December and we were married at the *Mairie,* or town hall, of the fourth arrondissement. Then we settled in, Marjie taking courses in French at a commercial academy on the place Saint-Michel and I doing my research.

{ 7 }

This meant spending long hours in one of the rare book rooms of the Bibliothèque Nationale. In the end, nothing came of those hours—there was simply not enough material for a thesis—but Marjie and I did manage to spend time discovering and enjoying Paris, whose charm (even during this protracted stay, which lasted for two years) remained as potent as ever.

A part of this charm was a certain archaic quality of the city, as compared to New York. As soon as World War II was over, New York had begun to race headlong into the second half of the century. Traffic doubled, crime tripled, television arrived. Lever House was built on Park Avenue, the first of a series of glass office towers that would eventually transform all of midtown Manhattan into a model of modernity for the whole world. Paris, however, for at least a decade after the war, remained as if suspended in a pre-War limbo, with many of its street scenes unchanged since the Belle Epoque. There were no new buildings, few new-model cars, almost no traffic lights or one-way streets. There were no televisions, frozen foods or supermarkets, and a refrigerator was a luxury. Telephone service was ridiculous. All of this reminded me of the Depression New York of my early childhood, when we had an icebox cooled by a big chunk of ice that was delivered once a week, when the Fifth Avenue buses that ran on Riverside Drive were double-decked, when nobody had a washing machine but every middle-class family had a maid.

The obverse of this charm was that everything was falling apart. Paris was then a dark-colored city, with the accumulated dirt of decades staining all building facades, except at certain corners where the wind-driven rain had created flashes of white stone. Once inside a front door controlled by an electric buzzer that often did not work, the halls and stairs of all buildings displayed worn carpets and peeling paint, with the odor of mildew rising from the basement. Electrical wiring was antiquated, and most homes displayed a whole vocabulary of little gadgets one could buy in the hardware store, reflecting the general penury: such as a *prise voleuse* (literally, a "thieving plug") for the gimmick you screwed into the light fixture over the sink to use your electric razor, assuming there was some daylight in your bathroom.

Heating in the winter was inadequate, partially because French architecture since the Renaissance has never faced the realities of the French climate north of the Loire. The style is all high ceilings and huge French windows, and when those windows have fifty years of accumulated paint on them, they never really shut. In the middle of winter there was a damp cold that permeated everywhere, be it your hotel room, the corner café or the local movie house—which often showed old American films, since the French had not yet completely caught up on all they had missed during the Occupation.

This gloomy ambiance is perfectly reflected in the theater of the period, notably the plays of Beckett and Ionesco, in which the characters find themselves in a shadowy limbo that makes any hope of improvement seem unreal and unrealistic. When these plays were put on in New York, they were characterized as the "Theater of the Absurd." In Paris at the time, they did not seem absurd at all, merely a distillation of life as it was lived every day. There is a play of Ionesco's called *Amédée, or How to Get Rid of It*. It's about a husband who has killed his wife's lover and left the body in the bedroom of the apartment, not knowing how to dispose of it, and who then notices that, instead of deteriorating, the body is growing larger day by day. The husband and wife have long arguments about their situation as the toes of a huge foot begin to invade their living room. The play was a great success, because every Parisian of the period could find, in this oppressive presence, something with which to identify.

This self-conscious gloominess, this assertion of despair, translated into an attitude of excessive and obvious reserve on the part of almost all Frenchmen when they met foreigners. Indeed, in our first year in Paris, my wife and I made not one French friend. It didn't matter too much, because then, as always, there was a large community of

{9}

foreigners in the French capital. And those expatriates, temporary or permanent, all shared a delicious little secret, an almost clandestine pleasure, which was the unstated, defiant conviction that despite all the gloom, Paris was simply the best place in the whole world to live.

This was a totally irrational belief and we all knew it, so that if anyone ever challenged the idea, citing the obvious defects in French character or society, the fact that things didn't work and that the French for the most part were hostile to foreigners, we would hasten to agree, reserving for ourselves the knowledge that all those rational objections were totally beside the point.

What then *was* the point? Part of it was the food, of course; almost no one has ever disputed French superiority in that department. No matter how many things were falling apart, your neighborhood restaurant never let you down. And there was much more difference between French food and American food back in the fifties than there is today. At that time, even in New York, endives or artichokes were found only in a few specialty shops; salad was iceberg lettuce, cheese was Velveeta. While in Paris the central market, les Halles, was still in the center of the city (it has since been moved to the town of Rungis). Almost everything was trucked in from the country, sold and re-sold, distributed to thousands of retail outlets or restaurants (most of them very small and specialized), cooked and consumed, all within twenty-four hours. And the results, even when the ingredients were very simple, could be surprising. To go to Le Chien qui Fume for a late supper, when the first trucks from the country were unloading their vegetables, to feast on snails in garlic butter with plenty of fresh bread, washed down with new Beaujolais—preferably Brouilly—direct from the barrel, made you forgive and forget a lot of dim light bulbs and drafty rooms.

Part of it was also the French language. If the French could be rudely intolerant of foreigners who made mistakes in pronunciation or grammar, they were at least partly excused by their love of the language itself, its particular concision, precision, and logic. In addition to the formal literary language, there was a huge vocabulary of not quite correct popular expressions, which everybody used when talking aloud, and there was also *argot*, that very French slang that is distinguished not for its vulgarity, but rather for its invention and poetry. In one of Ionesco's plays there is an exchange possible only in a country in which an awareness of the delights and constraints of the proper use of language is perpetually on everyone's mind: "All this is only words, words, words!" one character complains, to which another answers, "It's only the words that count! all the rest is only talk!"

And there is the beauty of the city. The beauty of Paris is not like that of New York or San Francisco; it is not a knock-out from anywhere. In fact, the more of Paris you see at one time the more of it you miss: the worst view of all is from atop the Eiffel Tower, from where Paris is only a big, sprawling city with a modest-sized river running though it. No, what really captivates is the late afternoon sun on the arches of rue de Rivoli, or the Eiffel Tower glimpsed diagonally through the rear window of a taxi, or a Gothic steeple at the end of a street as one comes up from the Metro, or the gentle curve of rue Saint-Antoine that saw the tumbrels of the Revolution. These are all things that native Parisians take for granted. But you need only to be from another country, or to have returned to another country, to admit that yes, these small vistas have become personally important.

And then there is living with history. But most of what follows will be about that.

ᏉᏉ   ᏉᏉ   ᏉᏉ

Now I'm going to jump forward almost thirty years, to 1982. In that time I had never been away long enough for Paris to become unfamiliar or foreign. Marjorie and I had been back for a long visit in 1958 and had kept in touch with the friends we had made earlier. After her death in 1964, I had come back a number of times alone, and after I remarried in 1975 those visits became annual, because my wife, Marianne, is French and her family lives in Paris.

Since we were spending more and more time each year in Paris, it seemed like a good idea to acquire an apartment there. For both of us this was emotional as well as practical; Paris was her home town and, by then, my oldest love affair. For all that the city had changed since those first two weeks in 1949, it still emanated a special aura for me.

I felt that aura each time I arrived, each time my taxi or the airport bus crossed the *périphérique* and entered the city. Coming from America, one generally arrives early in the morning, when Paris is just waking up. Suddenly, there it is: the confident apartment houses, the cafés and the *tabacs*, the lines of tightly pruned trees, the glistening pavements, the pale northern light, the trucks delivering kegs of beer, the newsstands, the diligent buses, the old ladies wearing faded shapeless dresses and rope slippers, a working man in faded blue cotton carrying a baguette as the street lights go out avenue by avenue. Nothing special; just what the French mean when they call their capital by its slang name: *Panam.*

Arriving that summer of 1982 had a new excitement because of the idea of perhaps making some corner of the city our second home. As it happened, Marianne had gone to Paris ahead of me; she had already been to see a couple of real estate agents and had a few places to show me by the time I arrived. With one exception, they were all in the district known as the Marais. This might have seemed accidental—we were staying in her parents' apartment in that neighborhood, and she had begun her search with what was close by—but in fact the Marais was the neighborhood where we most wanted to live, even though it had the reputation of having become the most expensive real estate in Paris. There is a charm to the Marais that is unique, but precisely because of that we knew that finding anything we could afford was going to be difficult.

And indeed, most of what Marianne had been shown was discouraging. The "remodeled studio with garden" turned out to be a ground floor room with a sink and hot plate, facing a narrow court. A "studio with exposed beams" was divided into cells by those very beams. A "68 square meters—bargain" had light and space but needed so much work that it would no longer be a bargain once the repairs were done. We were about to give up and wait for another occasion, when an agent to whom we were returning a key said there was a small duplex that she would like to show us if we didn't mind steps. It had already been sold but the contract had fallen through and the owners had just reduced the price.

We went right away. The apartment was in a nondescript building at the corner of rue Vieille-du-Temple and rue des Rosiers, the short street known for its kosher food shops. There were ninety-six steps up a very narrow staircase that turned twice for each floor. The previous client, a musician, had backed out of his contract when he found it was impossible to mount even a spinet piano. Then we reached the topmost landing, which was the *"cinquième"*—the "fifth floor" in French, which means "sixth" in the United States, since our "first floor" is their *rez-de-chaussée,* or ground floor. We caught our breath as the agent found the right key and opened the door. And then we walked in.

We found ourselves in a medium-sized room with some massive exposed beams and three windows that let in a generous flood of light from a great expanse of sky. The walls were painted white and the floor was covered by some ordinary beige carpeting. Marianne had walked in first and the first thing she did was to kick off her shoes, just like that, automatically, even as she was walking over to one of the windows to see what was outside.

What followed was only the details; I knew her decision had been made.

There was a bathroom and a kitchen off the living room. The bathroom was nicely done with blue tiles and new fixtures, but it had no window and no bidet. My wife had always complained of American bathrooms because they were small and sans bidet, but this time it did-n't seem to matter. The kitchen was only one meter by two but it did have a small window. There was a spiral staircase that led up to two narrow rooms, directly under the sloping roof so you could stand up in only half the area, but these little rooms were lit by modern skylights. The first was just large enough for a double-bed mattress and a small table. The second, which was smaller, could be a study or guest room, or so the agent suggested. "No," I answered, "it's going to be a walk-in closet." And then I realized that I, too, had made up my mind.

The fact of the matter is that we had both fallen in love with the place, but we kept our cool. We looked at everything very carefully, pretending to be critical; then we went back down the stairs and walked with the agent back to her office on rue de Turenne without saying any-thing. There she explained a bit more about what we had just seen.

The apartment was being sold by some *promoteurs*—i.e., "develop-ers"—who had gutted what had been two rooms occupied by a family of Tunisian immigrants plus the attic space overhead and redone everything. The agent said the drop in price had been substantial because, she thought, it was the end of July and the developers really wanted to sell and go off on their August vacations. But if we waited, the apartment would probably be snatched up by someone else.

It sounded just like what real estate agents always say, and yet the story was plausible in itself. So we told the young lady that we were definitely interested and would get back to her in the morning.

We then got on the phone and asked everyone we could reach if the price asked for the apartment was good or bad. And everyone said it was good. At last, we admitted to each other that we both wanted to go ahead with the deal, even if the apartment was a sixth-floor walkup.

In the morning we went back for a second look. The ninety-six steps were easier to climb the second time and the living room felt somewhat larger than it had the day before. The agent told us that the apartment was about fifty square meters (about 550 square feet), some of it unusable because of the sloping ceiling upstairs. But because the space was on two levels, it felt larger than that; wherever you were there was a room you couldn't see. And outside there were, undeniably, the rooftops of Paris. So we each took a deep breath and swallowed and nodded and then we went back to the office on rue de Turenne and signed a contract.

By the end of the day the contract had been accepted, and we had an appointment two days later to meet with the developers at the office of a notary—that inescapable French official who performs many of the functions of an attorney. The first step was signing a *promesse de vente*.

A *promesse de vente* is, roughly, a "letter of intent," and it is the crucial document in a sale. The title-search and other paperwork would delay the actual settlement for several months, but signing the *promesse de vente* meant that the apartment would be ours. As it happened, all we could offer as a deposit was a check on the Riggs Bank in Washington, DC, which according to French law the sellers could not deposit. This

*"…a nondescript building at the corner of
rue Vieille-du-Temple and rue des Rosiers…"*

didn't seem to matter to the *promoteurs,* who were three men in their forties, all from the south of France. They were indeed anxious to leave for their vacations; one even had his suitcases with him.

"We're not making anything on this deal," the one who seemed to be in charge assured me. "It was all a labor of love, something to pass the time. If you knew what problems we ran into!"

Again, that sounded just like what a developer would be expected to say, but then this was after the fact. In any event, only the notary seemed to care about the niceties of the documents and the fact that in France our check was just a piece of paper. We had their signatures and they had ours and everyone wanted to go to the beach.

Was this really Paris, the Paris of the *prise voleuse,* of Beckett and Ionesco? Yes and no; it was still Paris, but it was thirty years later and, as the fake doctor says in Molière's play, "All that has been changed!" This was again evident when the real estate agent cheerfully gave us the key to the apartment that was not yet ours, something that would not have been possible in the bad old days. And this access was important, since when you buy an apartment in France there is a lot missing that would already be in place in an apartment in the United States—such as light fixtures, a medicine cabinet in the bathroom, a stove, a refrigerator, and kitchen cabinets.

We had decided we wanted to order all these essentials, as well as some basic furniture, before we left in September. Since the rooms were so small we had to plot everything out on graph paper, counting every centimeter. So we went to the apartment every day, measuring and re-measuring; and then we went to the Bazar de l'Hôtel de Ville, or BHV (the best department store in Paris for household goods), which fortunately was only a few blocks away, to measure what we intended to buy, and then back to the apartment to measure once again.

We had an immediate deadline of sorts, because we had accepted an invitation to spend a week in the country beginning August 10th. By August 9, we had decided what we were going to order by way of a stove, refrigerator, and cabinets, and at eleven in the morning we made one more stop at the apartment just to check yet again that everything was going to fit. Then we left for the BHV.

It took longer than we had anticipated to place our orders, since each transaction involved a different salesperson and we had to explain each time that we wanted delayed delivery. Finally we reached the last item, the kitchen cabinets. The slip was all filled out, but the sales woman wanted to be sure that the cabinets we wanted were definitely in stock. She left us to go to a back office, and when she came back she was visibly upset.

"Your apartment is on rue des Rosiers?" she asked. Well, she had just heard on the radio that there had been a terrorist attack only moments ago on rue des Rosiers. She didn't know exactly what had happened, but several people had been killed.

The saleswoman's attitude toward us had suddenly changed; it was subtly different, as if she herself were somehow threatened or contaminated because she had written up an order to be delivered to rue des Rosiers.

We immediately left the store. As soon as we got outside we saw a line of the grey buses of the CRS, the special police who are called out for demonstrations or disasters. The streets leading north from rue de Rivoli toward rue des Rosiers were all blocked.

In the street people were talking to each other excitedly, agreeing only that whatever had happened had begun at Goldenberg's kosher restaurant in the middle of the street and that people had been killed. Taking the long way around by Bastille to avoid the blocked streets, we went back to where we were staying and turned on the radio. Many of the stations had scrapped their scheduled broadcasts and were reporting "live" about the *attentat*, but what we heard was a series of different reports, depending on the station. The air waves in France had only recently been made available to what were called *radios libres*, or non-state-run radio stations. There was the gay station, the North African station, the Jewish station, the Protestant station, and others, each with a cacophony of commentary and very few hard facts. It was only when the evening news was broadcast on television that we began to get some solid information as to what had actually happened a couple of blocks away.

It was the summer of 1982. The Israeli army had occupied West Beirut and emotions were heated all over the world by the issue of Israeli treatment of the Palestinians. This was especially true in France, with its large Jewish and Arab populations, its pro-Palestinian Leftist parties, and its anti-Semitic fanatics on the far Right. There was the somber record of bombings of synagogues and other Jewish establishments in the 1970s and other acts of violence involving Iranis and Libyans. So there were any number of groups who might be responsible for this latest act of terrorism.

What had happened was that at 12:30, only shortly after we had left the apartment for the BHV, two or three men with machine guns had gotten out of a car in front of Goldenberg's restaurant and begun firing. Three people were killed then and there, including a Moroccan Arab who had worked in the restaurant for twenty years. The terrorists then ran west on rue des Rosiers, shooting at random. Their victims numbered twenty-two wounded and three additional dead, including an American and a Belgian tourist. When they reached rue Vieille-du-Temple the assassins disappeared, probably driving off in another car that had been waiting for them.

The witnesses on the spot were able to add very few details since they had all been ducking for cover. But one man did report that one of the killers was smiling happily as he shot at whomever he saw. There is always some detail in the narration of a tragedy that seems to characterize the entire event; for me this was it. It recalls the poet André Breton's irresponsible statement that the purest Surrealist act is for a man to go down in the street and shoot passers-by at random. Perhaps he never expected anyone to take him literally.

PRESERVED BULLET HOLE IN THE WINDOW OF
GOLDENBERG'S RESTAURANT

The "responsibility" for this crime—as our unfortunate vocabulary
has it—has never been established. Whoever it was, the reaction in
France and in the world was so negative that no organization has ever
claimed "credit" for the butchery. As for Marianne and myself, for the
moment we were simply stunned. We had been living our little romantic dream of buying a pied-à-terre in Paris, and suddenly the violence
of History had intruded. Since we already had our train tickets for the
next morning, we did what was easiest, and simply carried on.

When we returned to Paris a week later, we brought with us four
small wooden chairs with straw seats that we had found in a country
shop, our first furniture for the apartment. There were no taxis at the
Gare de Lyon, so we took the chairs on the bus and went directly to rue
des Rosiers, then lugged them up the ninety-six steps. Nothing in the
neighborhood looked different, aside from the fact that there were
police all over. And yet we were a little apprehensive when the doorbell
rang shortly after we had arrived.

It turned out to be only a serious-looking young man who was a real estate agent, accompanied by a young woman who was moving to Paris and desperately wanted a little apartment in the Marais.

We told them that the apartment had been sold.

ക   ക   ക

Back in the fifties, when I lived in Paris, the Marais was not a place where I spent much time, even though for several months I was living on the Ile Saint-Louis, which is two steps away. The friends my wife and I made at that time lived either at Saint-Germain-des-Prés or in Montparnasse. When it came to marketing, the island itself still had its old village atmosphere, with inexpensive little shops on rue Saint-Louis-en-l'Ile. For anything more ambitious we went to the market at

"...wooden chairs with straw seats..."

{ 21 }

place Maubert, on the Left Bank. The guidebooks all said that the Marais was full of architectural marvels, but I didn't like the atmosphere of the place. I remember being disappointed by the place des Vosges, which was then seedy and covered with grime. And it was hard to discern the beauty of the historic mansions, since they were pitch black and often half obscured by dirty commercial signs. The whole neighborhood reminded me of the Lower East Side because of the push carts on rue Saint-Antoine and the signs in Yiddish on rue des Rosiers, as well as the faded laundry hung out the windows of overcrowded apartments. In short, it seemed little more than a worn-out slum.

And that is exactly how the municipal authorities of the time regarded the district. Certain areas had been declared *"îlots insalubres"* and condemned; their inhabitants had been moved out and the windows boarded up. This was not done out of malice; many of the old buildings were indeed "unhealthy," with crumbling walls, ceilings, and floors, make-shift arrangements for heat, inadequate and dangerous electrical wiring, and antiquated plumbing (if any at all). There was a certain smell to those buildings that is the universal stench of urban decay, an odor compounded of sweat, urine, mildew, and garbage. The only reason more of the Marais had not been condemned and emptied was a shortage of money to build replacement housing; there was no place to put the people who lived in the old, rotting apartments.

At that time, the plan was to preserve and restore a score or so of the historic buildings and turn them into schools, libraries, or government offices. Then everything else would be torn down and replaced with modern buildings set along streets that would be widened and straightened to accommodate automobile traffic. Some of these new buildings would be subsidized low-rent apartments for the former inhabitants of the area; others would be offices or middle-class housing. There were a few corners of the Marais where this vision had already become a reality, and they stand today as awful reminders of what would have become of the whole district if more funds had been available.

Along the Seine at the Pont Marie, which leads to the Ile Saint-Louis, there is a large, open area, formerly a crowded slum that had been declared an *"îlot insalubre"* as far back as 1919. Demolition in this district began after the war. Among the treasures of this *îlot* was the Hôtel de Sens, a rare example of medieval domestic architecture, built at the end of the fifteenth century. Its restoration was largely a reconstruction, since the fortress-like building had become so dilapidated; it now houses a library and exhibition space. Around it modern apartment houses were constructed in a gray stone that have acquired a pleasant patina; their proportions and roof lines, though undistinguished, imply a certain respect for the place where they are built. But their uniformity is a sad contrast to the variety of most of the Marais and the Hôtel de Sens now looks like a "Gothic" hall on an Ivy League campus.

Behind the Hôtel de Sens there is a small formal garden with very low clipped hedges, in a geometric pattern. Across rue des Nonnains-d'Hyères is a large flat space, occupied by a playground and a parking lot. Further to the west stands the Cité des Arts, a building that is vaguely "Bauhaus" in style, containing studios for foreign artists, opened in 1965 and recently renovated. It is not a bad building—if it were somewhere else—and for my wife and me the public parking garage in its basement is a great convenience. But it contributes to making the site soporific, despite the view of the Ile Saint-Louis across the Seine.

Still, we should not judge the municipal authorities, who would have redone all of the Marais in that way, too harshly. After all, there is nothing wrong with light and air and good sanitation. No, the greatest crime those authorities may have committed is a lack of imagination. They could not imagine doing anything with the Marais other than tearing it down and replacing it with something modern, because for them it was only a slum and it had never been anything more than a slum.

What finally happened to the Marais instead is a kind of a miracle. In 1958 Charles de Gaulle came back into power, and the following year he created a new cabinet post that had never before existed, the Minister

THE HÔTEL DE SENS

"…like a 'Gothic' hall on an Ivy League campus…"

of Culture, to which he appointed his long-term supporter, the writer André Malraux. Malraux, in addition to being a novelist, was a well-known art historian and a philosopher of history. When he became Minister of Culture, he was determined to be more than just an ornament of the new regime. His first proposal was to establish cultural centers in the principal provincial cities of France—the now-familiar *Maisons de la Culture*. French society had been highly centralized for centuries, and in no field was this truer than in the realm of the arts. Everything that was important happened in Paris, everyone who had any talent went to Paris, and what was left behind was "provincial" in the most negative sense of the word. Actually there had been efforts to decentralize the arts for decades, but Malraux proposed to back this up with a massive infusion of funds.

The new Minister then turned to the capital itself. Paris of the twentieth century had always been a city in grey and black, with a few dramatic flashes of white. It had been that way for so long that no one alive could remember it ever being any different. This was true not only of Paris: London, Brussels, and every other city of northern Europe where coal had been used for heating since the early nineteenth century were as black as if they were in perpetual mourning. What Malraux proposed was that the entire city, every building old and new, be cleaned.

There was an immediate outcry of shock and horror, as if the buildings had always been black, as if a century's accumulation of dirt were an historic patina of great artistic merit or the embedded soot were all that was holding the buildings up. But Malraux persisted, beginning with the structures owned by the government for which his ministry was responsible, such as the Louvre. Various methods of cleaning the old stones were tried; then it was discovered that the best was simply using steady streams of cold water without any soap or solvents.

It was hard to argue with a procedure that did nothing more than duplicate the effect of wind-driven rain. And when the canvases behind which the work had proceeded on the first buildings were taken down, the effect was stunning. There were stones that were a soft ocher, bricks that were a soft red, marble decorations of black and green; a whole palette of colors that had been hidden by the grime. And the untouched structures alongside no longer seemed to be coated with the dignity of age; they just looked dirty.

In the end, the entire city of Paris was cleaned. The effects were perhaps more visible in the Marais than anywhere else, because there was more in the way of beauty to be discovered beneath the grime. On the other hand, the process of cleaning went more slowly in the Marais. Old buildings classified as national monuments demand more care in their restoration than others. What was most important for the ultimate transformation was another law designed specifically for the Marais and

THE LOUVRE BEING CLEANED
"…the effect was stunning…"

other such districts all over France, the Law of 1962, generally known as the "Malraux Law."

As its name indicates, this also was an idea of the Minister of Culture. It established the principle of preserving and restoring not just isolated historic monuments, but entire districts or towns that had an historic character. This included many structures or facades that, had they been standing alone, would have had no particular interest. This is now standard practice in urban planning, but in 1964, when the Marais became the first such designated district in France, it was a revolutionary idea. And the effect was radical. The whole earlier program of bulldozing entire blocks to make way for modern buildings was revised so that each existing edifice was examined individually and then renovated instead of being demolished. If that was not possible, a facade would be saved; and if *that* was not possible, the new building would follow the roof line and general bulk of the district, instead of creating useless open space like a missing tooth.

It was then that the "private sector"—real estate entrepreneurs—began to get into the act. Everyone woke up to the fact that the Marais was part of the center of Paris, with buildings that it was impossible to reproduce anywhere and that it was now forbidden to tear down. Numerous American cities have seen the same process at work in districts like SoHo in New York, Georgetown in Washington, or the Battery in Charleston. The Marais had suddenly become fashionable.

For all that it was now officially an historic district, the Marais did not become a Parisian Williamsburg, with every structure restored to its original condition. That was neither possible nor desirable. To understand what *was* done, we can imagine, as an example, a typical seventeenth-century *"hôtel"*—a "mansion" or "city house"—and follow its evolution through the centuries.

The street out front would be fairly narrow, and along the sidewalk there would be a solid masonry wall, pierced at its center by a double door wide enough for a coach to enter: the *porte cochère*. If the *hôtel* is very grand, there might also be an arch, with perhaps a coat of arms carved on the keystone. Once through this gateway, you would find a cobblestoned courtyard, with probably a two-story structure to one side that houses a stable on the ground level and servants' quarters above. Just ahead is the house itself, three or four elegant stories high, often with additional rooms under a steep-pitched roof pierced with gables. The house, when you enter it, is not very deep, and often no greater in width than a large room; you notice immediately that there is a good-sized garden behind. The rooms all have very high ceilings and lead from one to another. Aside from the staircase and its landings there are no halls; there are also no closets, no bathrooms, no plumbing, and no heat aside from the fireplaces. Looking around at the way the house is laid out, it seems to have been built to be a museum. And indeed it is richly furnished with paintings, tapestries, carved paneling, and very fancy furniture—but it isn't a museum, although it may well become one three centuries later. The *hôtel* is the home of a seventeenth-century noble family with all its dependents and hangers-on.

We return a century later: Someone has built a cottage at the back of the garden, with smaller rooms than in the main house. Some of the rooms in the house itself have been subdivided, not only vertically but also horizontally, taking advantage of the high ceilings. There are now some halls; the place has been remodeled into several apartments and rented out.

On to the nineteenth century: the subdividing has progressed further. Holes have been cut in the wall facing the street to make shop fronts with dark dens constructed behind. The former servants' quarters are now let out as furnished rooms. Half the main house is now a *pension de famille;* the other half is rented to working-class families, room by room. The mistress of a banker is installed in the newly redecorated cottage behind the garden, which is often left untended.

We skip forward to the 1930s: One of the shops is a kosher butcher's establishment; the former courtyard is covered with a tin roof and

HÔTEL LIBÉRAL BRUANT
"...three or four elegant stories high..."

houses an automobile repair shop. The main house has some dingy offices on its first two floors; otherwise it is a warren of furnished rooms. The garden is now just a patch of dirt with an outhouse, the cottage houses a sweat shop where underpaid women spend their days sewing overalls on antiquated sewing machines.

And today: After a careful renovation, under the watchful supervision of six government agencies, the garden is a garden once again. The cottage is still there, restored to its eighteenth-century charm. The shop out front now sells Mexican tiles. There is an electric security system to open the right-hand door of the *porte cochère* that leads from the street to the courtyard. The main house and its dependencies, all cleaned and redone, are now ten apartments, four of them studios, the rest with parquet floors and exposed wooden rafters—which were of course concealed behind plaster when the house was originally built. The owners include a television producer and an internationally known movie star.

This is a hypothetical example. The Marais is a good-sized neighborhood and all the buildings are not yet even cleaned; the process is still going on. In 1982, my wife and I, by buying a renovated apartment formerly occupied by Tunisian immigrants, had become part of it.

❧ ❧ ❧

In the few weeks that remained of that summer, we did as much as we could to furnish the apartment; then it was time to go back to America. An aunt of Marianne's signed for us at the settlement, which took place in October, then mailed us all the papers. They were a thick dossier of documents tracing the ownership of the apartment back to the day in 1967 when the building had become a condominium. As is usual in French documents, there were many details that would not be found in their American equivalents—the places and dates of birth of the previous owners, their nationality and marital status, including dates of marriage and divorce where applicable. The papers were clearly in order.

We returned to Paris the following spring, going directly from the airport to our own place for the first time. A young friend had lived in the apartment during the winter in return for taking delivery of what we had ordered and installing the kitchen equipment. The one hitch had been the refrigerator. The refrigerator we had ordered at the Bazar de l'Hôtel de Ville the day of the terrorist attack was not, he had been informed, available with a left-hinged door. In our narrow kitchen this was a crucial detail. So he had canceled the order and found another model in another store that would fit in the limited space under the hot water heater. But it was not "frost free." Nothing is ever perfect.

One thing that had worried me about the apartment was the stairs, all ninety-six of them, leading up from the street. I had visions of having to plan my days very carefully to come and go as little as possible. But once there, I found the stairs were not a problem. Instead, after a few weeks, if I wanted a fresh *baguette* for breakfast, I would slip on some clothes and run down to buy it, not at the first but at the second bakery on rue Vieille-du-Temple because the bread was better there.

That is the kind of distinction you find yourself making when you live in the center of Paris. We discovered that our own particular corner of the Marais was very different from what we had known before when we had stayed with my father-in-law near the place des Vosges. Rue des Rosiers ended right at our corner, which meant that close by there were shops and bakeries specializing in smoked salmon, taramasalata, stuffed vine leaves, halvah, challah, bagels, and other Jewish and Near Eastern delicacies. Rue des Rosiers is a tourist attraction of sorts, so there were stands selling falafel and a snack bar offering "Kosher Fast Food." There was a book shop specializing in Jewish history, another with Israeli magazines and newspapers; also several traditional kosher butchers and grocers. During the week the street was crowded with trucks; on Saturdays everything was closed; on Sundays, when everything was open, the street was often completely blocked by cars with suburban license plates, as nostalgic people who grew up in the neighborhood returned for a taste of their childhood.

But with everything changing so rapidly, even rue des Rosiers had become mixed. A restaurant now featured kosher Vietnamese food; there was a fashionable tea room and several boutiques featuring the clothes of young designers. And when you turned left from the door of our building, it was a very different kind of neighborhood. There was the long-established gay bar called the Hotel Central, in addition to a gay book shop, a gay tea room, and several gay discotheques. There were (and still are) four or five *café théâtres*, each offering five or six shows per evening in small performance spaces with minimal stages. The shows were usually comic skits, occasionally with something ambitious, such as a parody of Racine. There were art galleries, antiques shops, two stores selling only bonsai, two or three wine bars, and several bookstores. And also, as all over Paris, an assortment of restaurants, ranging from cheap couscous joints to expensive establishments offering updated traditional French cuisine.

In the summer of 1982, when we bought our apartment, there had been a snack bar open twenty-four hours a day on the street level at the corner of rue des Rosiers and rue Vieille-du-Temple. This was under the same management as a night club called the Chevaliers du Temple, which had been known as a jazz spot in the early seventies. By the time we returned the following spring, both the snack bar and the night club were closed. The cellars that housed the nightclub are reached by a staircase down from rue des Rosiers. The first time I went down those stairs was after the nightclub had gone out of business, and this descent came as something of a revelation.

There were two levels, both covered with vaults of roughly hewn stone, plus some nooks and crannies off to the sides. In the passageway between the two areas was what remained of a circular well, although you didn't hear a splash if you dropped something down. The air was cool and rather damp. The two spaces would have made a great bomb shelter but were rather awkwardly arranged for a nightclub, which is perhaps why the space was still vacant. But it was all clearly very, very old.

As for the building itself, the earliest date in the sale documents was sometime in the nineteenth century, although by all appearances it must have been much older. This is not surprising since official records in France go back no further than the reign of Napoleon, everything before the Revolution being considered ancient history, with no legal standing. The real estate agent figured the building dated at least from the seventeenth century and this, from my American point of view, seemed quite old enough. But now I began to suspect that it was not at all old enough.

I had become very familiar with the ninety-six narrow steps that turn between each floor as you go up. Now I looked at them more carefully, and also at the other staircase that goes up to the apartments at the back of the building. A few blocks away on rue François-Miron, there

"…two houses constructed in the fifteenth century…"

are two houses that a plaque proclaims were constructed in the fifteenth century. They have facades of exposed timbers, of the kind that we tend to label Elizabethan but are actually typical of domestic Medieval architecture found all over northern Europe. They have been restored, and the front doors are locked. But if you manage to get into the hall to examine the stairs, they turn out to be identical to the ones in our building. Only in their general form, of course; everything has been redone and redone again over the centuries.

THE STAIRCASE, RUE DES ROSIERS
"...identical to the ones in our building..."

{ 34 }

Just across rue François-Miron there was the headquarters of the Festival du Marais. Inside were several shelves of books about the neighborhood, and one of them was an unfinished historical inventory of all the buildings in the district.* I had been there before, but now, propelled by a growing curiosity, I went in and looked up our building.

There was not very much, but the date of the first entry was 1393. It gave the names of the owners of 33 rue des Rosiers—"the house at the sign of 'St. Julien' belonged to Robin Pasquier"—and of 35 rue des Rosiers—"Hennart de Cambenart, Usher to the King"—who also owned the house at 38 rue Vieille-du-Temple. (These are the original three houses that probably were built joined together as one average-sized building with a common foundation and basement.)

So there it was, three centuries older than we had been told. Now according to the "Malraux Law," our building is only one of those *"habitations d'accompagnement"*—an ordinary house that should be preserved only because in its proportions and general character it fits in with the neighborhood. From my American point of view this seemed strange—an "ordinary" house that dated back to at least 1393. But then I reflected that, in the context of the Marais, yes, this house was of interest only as part of the ensemble—it was a bit player on the architectural stage. After all, it had been built as an ordinary house—or rather three ordinary houses—with no particular architectural distinction. No one of any historical importance had ever lived there. Its only extraordinary attributes were that it had been built well enough to last six centuries and that it was where it was—at that corner in the Marais.

It was then that my curiosity was aroused, and I began to read everything I could find about the history of the Marais, and especially whatever could help me imagine the lives of the people who had lived at that particular street corner through the centuries. And I did find a

* Catherine Cournaud, *Le Marais* (Paris: Société des Gens de Lettres, 1980). The same building is now the headquarters of the Paris Historical Society.

PASSAGE DES SINGES, BY ATGET

"...a nest of criminals..."

great deal about the Marais, and that our "ordinary house" had witnessed any number of interesting events. In 1410—this was during the Hundred Years War—the Duke of Orléans, brother of the king of France, was assassinated one block away. In the eighteenth century, Beaumarchais wrote *The Marriage of Figaro* in a house just across the street. In the nineteenth century, when the neighborhood had really deteriorated, the Passage des Singes—again just across the street—was a nest of criminals, and was later photographed by Atget. In 1942, German soldiers rounded up all the students of a Jewish school just around the corner, loaded them onto buses, and deported them to Auschwitz. And in 1982, there was the terrorist attack at Goldenberg's on rue des Rosiers.

But for most of the six or seven hundred years since the ordinary house was built, it had been occupied by a succession of anonymous people, many of whom had been completely by-passed by the great events around them. I would have liked to have discovered, or uncovered, all their stories, no matter how banal or fragmentary. But that, I soon realized, was not possible.

Still, I was lucky enough to find the records of one family who had lived at this corner in the Marais about midway between the time when the house was built and the present day; a single family whose existence had never been of interest to anyone else. These records were legal documents, and like most legal documents they were abstruse and incomplete. But in the course of locating them, and then of consulting studies that helped me understand them, I was convinced that there would be considerable reliable background information available for every period since the house was first constructed. And so we are permitted to imagine, without feeling it is only imagination, how this ordinary house came to be built, how it was built, and who might have lived in and around it at various times. That is the kind of information that is called "History"—the sum of all we know, and infer, in the present about the past.

The Past…

ABOUT TEN THOUSAND YEARS AGO, the Seine cut through a narrow neck of dry land near what is now the eastern end of the Ile Saint-Louis to flow in what had previously been the bed of a small tributary stream, the Bièvre. The former path of the Seine then became a flood-prone plain on the Right Bank. This former river bed remains visible in the urban fabric even today, beginning with the Canal Saint-Martin from the Seine to Bastille and then continuing with a succession of boulevards and avenues all the way to the place de l'Alma. It was the eastern part of this flood-prone land, eventually drained and used for agriculture and then built over with houses and streets, that later gave the Marais—"the Marsh"—its name. And there is a certain poetic justice to the fact that this Marais was preserved, during the vigorous and destructive nineteenth century, by becoming an urban backwater.

The old Gallo-Roman town, Lutetia Parisiorum, was built mostly on the Left Bank, with its Forum on the hill of Saint-Geneviève (site of the current Panthéon). But during the violent centuries that followed the fall of Rome, the descendants of the Lutetians retreated to the Ile de la Cité in the middle of the river, which was a more defensible site. And when peace finally returned, the city began to grow back to its former size, with most of its expansion on the Right Bank, centered around the Châtelet—a medieval fort, long since vanished—just across the northern arm of the river from the Royal Palace on the Ile de la

Cité. This became the commercial center of the city, with its wharves, markets and money changers.

This Paris of the tenth and eleventh centuries still included considerable farmland within its boundaries, including the site that later became the rue des Rosiers. At the end of the twelfth century, the King known as Philippe Auguste, who had a penchant for fortifications, ordered the construction of the first stone wall around Paris, beginning on the Right Bank. This wall was a massive defensive structure, with circular towers every two hundred feet, so that the entire perimeter could by covered by archers. There were, on the Right Bank, only five or six gates through the wall, which, of course, were shut tight at night.

The existence of the wall quickly made the land inside it more valuable. Paris continued to grow; many new streets with building lots were created, involving numerous transactions between royal and municipal authorities and also between the churches and monasteries that owned most of the now enclosed agricultural land.

Actually it was not as simple as that. The word "created" covers a period of seventy-five years, and to say "owned" in relation to land is an anachronism: our modern notion of real property developed much later. In the Middle Ages the churches and monasteries did not own their land; they had been granted rights to it, very often by the Crown. And now that the land was valuable for more than growing wheat or cabbages, the Crown demanded part of the profits. So a good deal of legal redefinition had to be done before development could proceed.

The new street that interests us is one that ran east from rue Vieille-du-Temple until it reached the wall. Between this new street and the wall to the north there was a narrow strip of vacant land too shallow for building lots. Tradition has it that this strip was planted with rose bushes. Maybe these were planted by whatever institution finally got the right to lay out the new building lots on the south side of the street, perhaps the Church of Saint-Gervais. But one way or another, the new street was called "rue des Rosiers."

The houses built on this new street were unpretentious and the people who moved into them were equally modest: artisans, masons, cloth finishers. No names that have come down in history. The street was, after all, at the edge of the city and faced a massive barrier of crudely cut stones, three or four stories high that, even with the rose bushes, was not much to look at. The tallest of the houses themselves were perhaps as high as the wall, although most of them were undoubtedly smaller.

To modern eyes, this new street would look quaint and picturesque. The exteriors of the houses were crisscrossed half timbers and stucco, the slate roofs steep and gabled, the windows small and irregular. The whole street would have had a kind of crazy-quilt, jumbled look. But these were not facades in an amusement park; indeed the external appearance of the houses was certainly low on the list of priorities of their builders, compared to those of later centuries. The facades, however, did reveal or at least indicate something of the structure within. And that suggestion merits closer examination.

The great architecture of medieval France was the style later known as "Gothic," an architecture of stone that appears almost perversely to defy the innate qualities of its material, soaring and arching and opening to a lacework filled with the brilliance of stained glass; an architecture that was developed for churches, abbeys and cathedrals. For ordinary houses, however, stone, though widely available, was too expensive to be used as the prime material. And apart from the cost, in a northern climate where heating is necessary for at least half the year, stone houses can prove very uncomfortable. Nor was wood a solution: aside from the danger of fire, building-quality lumber was also expensive, the great forests of Roman times having long since disappeared. And so what was discovered or developed or evolved—any of those verbs will do to mask the fact that there are no documents—was a form of domestic architecture that we call the "half-timbered house." This structural style was to become the norm for most structures of the northern European cities over a period of centuries.

There is nothing particularly complicated about this sort of structure, which was designed by anonymous builders. Essentially these were a very solid wood-frame houses with walls formed of rubble held in place by mortar. These walls were finished—usually—with plaster on the inside and stucco on the outside, then topped off with a peaked roof of tiles or slate supported by a wooden scaffold.

The construction began with excavating one or two basements depending on the level of the water table; then covering them with vaults crudely cut stone. In Paris, on the Left Bank near the Seine, you run into water when you go down only a few feet; basements there are usually only one level deep or else non-existent. On the Right Bank however, inside Philippe Auguste's wall, it was possible to dig much deeper without running into ground water. Paradoxically, it is the Right Bank that has natural springs and good well water if you dig deep enough.

Our house on rue des Rosiers thus has two levels of cellars, which is what permitted the nightclub. The vaulting in those cellars is crude, vaguely Gothic, purely utilitarian. There is also the remnant of a well, a circle of stones going down twenty feet or so and dry at the bottom. The location of this "well" is such that at one time it might have been accessible from the little open courtyard above. That would certainly have been a plus for the inhabitants of the building; otherwise they would have had to carry their buckets to the nearest fountain, several blocks away, or buy river water from street peddlers.

Having finished the cellars and covered them with a good stone floor for the ground level, the builders then continued with masonry for two or three feet above the level of the street, leaving spaces for the doors; there they installed smooth stone thresholds. The first horizontal beams of the wood frame were posed on top of this masonry foundation, two inches or so in from the perimeter. It is to these beams, the *sabliers*, that the most important vertical beams were attached, the *gros poteaux* that would eventually support the house. In that way, the wood frame did not touch the ground, and was protected from humidity, termites and eventual decay. Any good modern builder knows these procedures and would follow them.

These vertical members, "the big posts," had been chosen with care and were probably the most expensive parts of the whole structure. They were of well seasoned hardwood, probably oak, and at least a foot square, probably thicker. They were as straight as could be found, but not like timbers cut by a mechanical saw; they were hand-hewn. They were as tall as necessary, depending on the number of stories the house was to be, since it was preferable that they go all the way up to the roof eaves. To the house, they were as the keel to a ship.

Attached to these corner posts were other timbers, first horizontal, then vertical, not quite as massive but still extremely solid, compared to those of a modern wood-frame house. These days we don't build four- or five-story wood-frame houses that will last for centuries. When we want strength we use steel or reinforced concrete; when it is a wood frame, we build airy cages with cardboard walls stuffed with glass wool for insulation, clothed in shingles to look rustic or brick to look solid, both of which will blow away in the next tornado. But in the Middle Ages, even when using wood, they built to await the Second Coming.

The framework being complete, the builders then constructed the chimneys, with fireplaces on each floor, at least one to every apartment, since it was fireplaces that served for both heating and cooking. These were of stone or brick or the two together. The walls came afterward, thicker at the bottom of the house and thinner above. The walls were not really supporting walls—since it was the wood frame that held up the house—but they were not curtain walls either. Held in place by wooden lathes, the walls added to the solidity of the whole. I suspect they functioned as much to hold the house down as to hold it up. The walls below held up the walls above and all the walls held the essential structure in place. It was an architecture of redundancy, the kind of over-building that serious people do when they don't know precisely what they're doing, which is why so many older buildings are still standing.

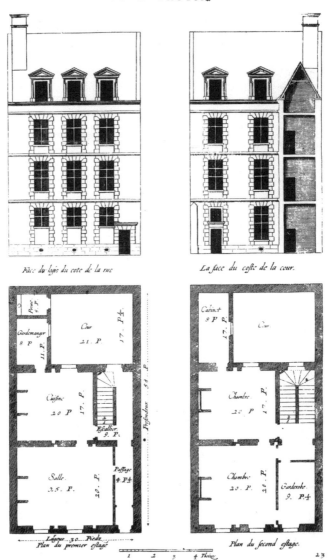

Face du logis du cote de la rue

La face du costé de la cour.

Plan du premier estagé

Plan du second estage.

23

TWO PLATES FROM PIERRE LE MUET'S
'MANIÈRE DE BIEN BASTIR' (1647)

1   2   .   Toize.

As for carpentry, the roof was the most complicated part of the entire edifice. But there were experts in roofing; even in the stone cathedrals, above the vaults visible from within, there was a massive wooden structure that held up the roof visible from without. This was also the most vulnerable component of the structure, the part that in a cathedral might be set on fire by lightning.

Last of all came the exterior. The easiest solution would have been to daub stucco over everything, but usually the builders left the vertical, horizontal and diagonal supporting and bracing timbers exposed, creating the characteristic facade by which we still recognize a half-timbered house.

And so our house was built, along with the others facing the wall on rue des Rosiers. But for this description of the construction of a medieval house, I must admit that I have anachronistically followed the procedures recommended in a work from the seventeenth century, Pierre le Muet's *Manière de bien bastir*, a "how-to" book published four centuries after the house at the corner of rue des Rosiers and rue Vieille-du-Temple was constructed. The reason for relying on this work is that it is the only document I have been able to locate that even partially explains the construction of a half-timbered house. And this leads us to the story of another ordinary house in the Marais, the house at 3 rue Volta, about half a mile north of rue des Rosiers, toward place de la République.

This typical example of the half-timbered house was described in my old *Guide Bleu* as "said to be fourteenth century and the oldest house in Paris." Now, its very location must have been what made the *Guide Bleu* cautious, since it stands well outside the trace of Philippe Auguste's wall and is not at all the kind of house that would have been built when that part of Paris was still half rural. What has since been discovered is that the house at 3 rue Volta was built in the seventeenth century by someone who followed the instructions in Le Muet's manual, perhaps someone with an antiquarian frame of mind who wanted a house to look as if it were already very old.

Rue des Rosiers turns up on some of the maps made by modern historians who have investigated the history of medieval Paris as belonging to what was called the *"Ville Neuve du Temple"*—i.e. the new streets laid out by the rich and powerful Knights Templar, whose headquarters had originally been near the Seine and who had since moved to a site outside the wall.* But whether rue des Rosiers was part of the Templar's domain or belonged to the church of Saint-Gervais, as some of the documents imply, is of little importance. What is clear is that the street did not exist until the thirteenth century.

In the new neighborhood around rue des Rosiers, the streets were quite wide for the period—eight yards—and laid out in an almost rectangular grid. If the street map is not perfectly regular, this is perhaps explained by the eventual incorporation of some old thoroughfares, such as rue Vieille-du-Temple, for which they probably bent the alignments here and there to accommodate existing buildings. Straight lines and strict right angles were not especially important to the medieval mentality, but by comparison to the older parts of the city, rue des Rosiers and the other streets laid out at the time, both inside and outside the wall, were almost as geometrically square as those of the new towns (*bastides*) built by Saint Louis in the south of France.

The contrast between this neighborhood and the older parts of the Right Bank is hard to imagine when you walk around modern Paris, since most of these older sectors were among those completely swept clean of anything of historic interest by Baron Haussmann in the nineteenth century. On the Ile de la Cité, where post-Roman Paris began, only Notre Dame and the Sainte Chapelle remain to testify to the genius and spirit of the Middle Ages, and even those monuments have

---

* This accounts for the fact that there are *rue Vieille-du-Temple* and *rue du Temple* only a few blocks apart: the first began at the original "Temple" behind Saint-Gervais, the second led to the more recent monastery, located near the modern place de la République on the site of the square du Temple.

THE HOUSE AT 3 RUE VOLTA
"...said to be the oldest house in Paris..."

been so completely transformed by the "restorations" of Viollet-le-Duc as to be almost as much examples of nineteenth century Romantic architecture as of medieval Gothic. In the Middle Ages, there was no open square in front of Notre Dame, and no park beside and behind the cathedral; indeed there was no place from which you would have a "view" of the monument at all. Houses crowded up close on all sides, fronting on narrow, irregular streets. This same maze of short, narrow streets continued on the Right Bank, which was the commercial heart of the city, crowded, noisy and no doubt quite dirty. Aside from two fairly straight streets heading north, rue Saint-Martin and rue Saint-Denis, and an open square in front of the town hall, every passageway was narrow and crooked. The upper stories of many houses extended so far out they almost touched, so there were many spots where the sun never reached the ground. With the press of pedestrians, street vendors, carts, horses and other animals, the traffic jams of medieval Paris were famous; there is a story, probably not apocryphal, of a country bumpkin in the days of Saint Louis who spent an entire Saturday trying to get across a bridge.

If by some miracle we were able to visit that core of the city as it was then, it would probably seem to us more like the "casbah" of a North African town than a European city. And indeed descriptions of the street scene of the period seem somehow "Oriental," with the variety of costumes, the stalls open directly on the street, the peddlers, the beggars, the jugglers and story tellers, and the colorful and passionate processions on religious holidays.

By contrast, rue des Rosiers and the other new streets would seem more familiar to us. These streets were wider and relatively straight, and the houses did not block out the sky. By the standards of any time and place, this was healthy and comfortable middle-class housing. Its builders may not have planned to build for the centuries, but I suspect that they would not have been surprised to learn they had.

Incidentally, the house was not yet in the Marais, for the simple reason that the word was not yet in use. That was to come a few centuries later, when people began to build mansions beyond the wall, on the site of the former river bed; after which the name was extended back to cover the eastern part of medieval Paris. And the *cinquième étage*, where the developers created our pied-à-terre in the sky, had not yet been built. That, too, was to come later.

಄಄   ಄಄   ಄಄

Having built our ordinary house, so to speak, we are now going to rush forward through the following two centuries, since the neighborhood, and presumably the building also, remained physically unchanged for quite a long time. What did change, and quite drastically, were the times: the social, political and environmental climate.

The thirteenth century, when the house was built, had been largely a period of growth and prosperity, the culmination of a certain form of civilization, epitomized by Notre Dame and Chartres cathedrals, the creation of the University of Paris, and the Crusades. By contrast the fourteenth and fifteenth centuries saw disasters on a scale that were not again equaled until our own times. These were the centuries of the Black Death and what we now call the Hundred Years War. Both of these left their mark on the city of Paris, but more for what did not happen than for anything that did. There were almost no notable buildings and no more new neighborhoods; the growth of the city came to a halt.

The Black Death—the bubonic plague, probably originating in Asia and spread by rats—ravaged all of Western Europe in a series of successive waves, in some regions reducing the overall population by a third or even a half. Paris never suffered unduly, but neither was it exempt. The plague first appeared in 1323, then in 1327, followed by particularly virulent episodes in 1348 and 1349. This last outbreak resulted in a shortage of laborers so severe that there were regulations requiring all healthy men to work full-time and freezing wages at a certain maximum.

The second half of the fourteenth century was relatively plague-free, but then the war began, with fighting in and around Paris. And then in the fifteenth century the plague returned. There was starvation, an emigration of the desperately poor; there were abandoned houses and gangs of marauding thieves, while outlying parts of the city reverted to country. Wolves were seen in Paris in 1421 and 1423, then again in 1438 and 1439, with reports of fourteen persons being devoured. In 1433 and 1445 there were smallpox epidemics that killed countless children, and another outbreak of the plague in 1448, an epidemic that reportedly left 50,000 dead.

Of course these events seem particularly dramatic when related in this compressed manner. In our own century we have seen just how resilient cities can be after comparable disasters. At times the surviving poor were better off than before due to lower rents, cheaper food, and higher wages. During this period Paris always attracted immigrants from more devastated regions, sometimes encouraged by royal tax exemptions for merchants and artisans. So after each decline the population soon rebounded to its earlier level.

As for the Hundred Years War—which was a series of small, bitter conflicts that went on and on—if the final result had been otherwise Paris would not have become the city we know today. For us the word "war" usually evokes a conflict between nations, and so we think of the Hundred Years War as between England and France, which, all in all, is what it became toward its end, when Joan of Arc launched her crusade to *"boutez les Anglais hors de France."* But for most of its duration the war was the expression of complicated dynastic rivalries, plus a good deal of opportunistic plundering by local warlords. This created alliances with little regard for national, or even local, loyalties, political bonds that hardly mattered at the time in any case.

But ultimately it was this prolonged chaotic conflict that resolved an important question: namely, just where the major power centers of Western Europe would be located and who would control them. It was no foregone conclusion at the time that later there would be a great unilingual nation called France with Paris as its capital. Instead there might have been a bilingual United Kingdom, based in London, incorporating Normandy, Brittany and Gascony as well as the British Isles. And there might have been a great multilingual nation including the rest of northern France plus Belgium with some good chunks of Germany thrown in. Dijon, to pick one of the candidates, might have become the capital of this Greater Burgundy and would now be a major European city. And if that had been the result of the Hundred Years War, Paris today would be another charming provincial city, like Dijon.

But it didn't turn out that way. Even when the English were finally back on their island, with the exception of the enclave they kept at Calais, the French kings did not settle down in their capital for any long periods of time. Partially this was due to fear, both of the plague and of the Parisians, who had never been the most loyal of subjects. Partially it was due to habit: military campaigns had kept the court wandering from castle to castle for decades. And so for two centuries Paris lost the preeminence that had made it grow, and it was often not even the political center of what was gradually evolving into the nation of France.

The sixteenth century began as more of the same, although Paris shared in the general French economic upturn due to domestic peace. François I, one of the colorful monarchs who left their stamp on the great Renaissance century, became king in 1515. During the first thirteen years of his reign he was rarely in Paris; instead he was off fighting in Italy, where he fell in love with the style of architecture we call "Renaissance" and where he was eventually taken prisoner by the forces of the Hapsburg Emperor Charles V. His ransom was French renunciation of claims to Burgundy, Flanders, and Artois. On his return from captivity, François decided to make Paris his principal

THE BASTILLE
"...a large fort at the end of rue Saint-Antoine..."

residence. On March 15, 1528, he sent a letter to the municipal authorities announcing that, "our intention is that from now on we will spend our time in our good city of Paris."

Which was not precisely the truth, since François was too attached to Fontainebleau, the royal palace only thirty miles from Paris, which he enlarged and transformed in the new Renaissance style. But François I also began the rebuilding of the Louvre, the military fortress that Philippe Auguste had built at the western end of his wall more than three centuries before. He tore down the *donjon* and had the place redecorated for the visit of his captor, the Emperor Charles V. He then commissioned the architect Pierre Lescot to design a new wing, of course in the latest Renaissance style. But the work had just begun when this ambitious, learned, and forward-looking monarch died.

The reign of François I also marked a change in the Marais. The north side of rue des Rosiers, that area planted with rose bushes between the wall and the street, had always been part of the royal domain. In need of money, as was usually the case with the kings of France, François had what remained of the wall torn down, divided the area between rue des Rosiers and rue des Francs-Bourgeois into building lots, and sold them off. His profitable real estate operation occurred in 1543, suggesting that once again the city was prosperous and growing. From rue des Rosiers, it was now at least as far to where the countryside began as to Notre Dame.

But in fact, the house at the corner had not been at the real edge of the city even when it was built; by the end of the thirteenth century there were already substantial neighborhoods outside the wall of Philippe Auguste. A century after its construction, so many gateways

Massacre de la S.ᵗ Bartholomi

THE SAINT BARTHOLOMEW'S DAY MASSACRE
"...the Seine, according to legend, ran red with blood..."

had been cut through the wall that it was useless from a military stand-point. In 1357, twenty years after the start of the Hundred Years War, there had been a short-lived Parisian insurrection against royal authority led by Etienne Marcel. This episode is seen by some historians as a distant precursor of the French Revolution. On this occasion, Marcel's forces dug a line of trenches that enclosed the real city as a defense against the royal army. But Marcel was assassinated by royalist sympathizers and the revolt was soon put down.

Thirteen years later, King Charles V constructed a new wall along Marcel's line of defense. Its most notable feature was a large fort at the end of rue Saint-Antoine, strategically placed to defend the city against any invaders who might arrive from the east. This was the Bastille.

The old wall, however, was not immediately demolished. Instead it was sold off in bits and pieces over time—the towers sometimes incorporated into houses and some of the stone used as walls for new buildings. This is why there are remains of Philippe Auguste's wall still standing today. But most of it was eventually demolished, its main use providing stones for building.

Shortly after the new wall was finished, Charles V built a country residence in the shadow of the Bastille, the Hôtel Saint-Paul, of which there is no trace today aside from the name of a street. This was replaced by the more extensive Hôtel des Tournelles, built about a century later. It was there that the son of François I, Henri II, lived during most of his twelve-year reign. During this time, the Louvre was a construction site. Adjacent to the Hôtel des Tournelles, at the end of rue Saint-Antoine, there was a large open space that was used for tournaments, those chivalric competitions that were the period's sport of kings. It was during one of these dangerous events that in March 1559 Henri II was mortally wounded by his opponent. His widow, Catherine de Médicis, had the palace torn down shortly afterward. Again, all that remains today is the name of a street.

François II became king after the death of Henri II, but his reign was brief, lasting only a year. In 1560 Catherine de Médicis became Regent, since her son Charles IX was then a minor. As everyone knows, it was Catherine de Médicis who ruled France during the reigns of her two younger sons, first Charles IX and then Henri III. This was the period of the Wars of Religion between Catholics and Protestants, a conflict further complicated and exacerbated by dynastic rivalries since none of Catherine's sons left any male heirs. The Queen Mother played off one side against another, always in the interest of reinforcing the power of the throne, and generally in the interest of the Catholic factions. It was she who planned the Saint Bartholomew's Day massacre, during which the Protestant leader Coligny was murdered and the Seine, according to legend, ran red with blood.

The royal court, which had never been more frivolous, was often outside Paris during her reign. But the seat of what can now be called the French state remained in the capital. And during this period, the latter half of the sixteenth century, the first of the sumptuous city residences that remain the distinctive monuments of the Marais were built.

We usually think of the Marais as an aristocratic neighborhood, but in fact most of the new buildings, designed in the Renaissance style, were constructed by government officials or Italian bankers, the latter brought to Paris through the Medici connection. Most of the open land between the medieval city and the wall of Charles V was by then divided up into building lots. The lots were usually between 4,000 to 7,000 square feet, a generous size for a town house, but the more impressive mansions were built on two or three of these lots. The Hôtel Carnavalet was built by a judge in 1546. The mansion at what is now 8 rue Elzévir was built by a royal official in 1575; the Hôtel Savourny on the same street was built by an Italian in 1586. On rue des Francs-Bourgeois, the year 1585 saw the construction of the Hôtel Mortier, built for a royal official; the same year saw the construction of the residence of Diane d'Angoulême (a real aristocrat, for once), a great house later known as the Hôtel de Lamoignon and now the Historical

HÔTEL DE DONON (MUSÉE COGNACQ-JAY), 1575
"...some far from ordinary neighbors..."

MEDIEVAL HOUSE IN A COURTYARD, RUE ELZÉVIR

Library of the city of Paris. On rue Vieille-du-Temple, just a few steps north of rue des Rosiers, the rich Italian merchant Ludovic Adjacet built himself a luxurious mansion that was to be known by the end of the century as the Hôtel d'O. So during those years that the history books suggest were all civil war and massacres, the house at the corner in the Marais had begun to acquire some far from ordinary neighbors.

When the second of Catherine's sons was assassinated in 1589, the man with the clearest title to the throne was Henri of Navarre, of the house of Bourbon, who was the leader of the Protestant forces. His ascension to the throne was opposed by the Ligue, a Catholic faction allied with Spain, which had its own candidate for king. But by then a large number of Frenchmen were fed up with civil war. There was growing support for those prominent individuals, both Catholic and Protestant, who preached tolerance and compromise, and who became known as *"les politiques."* With their support, Henri of Navarre decided to become a Catholic, reportedly murmuring, "Paris is worth a Mass." The legendary phrase reveals just how important the capital had become.

Negotiations took some time, but Henri of Navarre was consecrated as King Henri IV in Chartres in 1593—since Rheims, the traditional site for the French equivalent of a coronation, was controlled at the time by the Ligue. Henri IV then moved on to Paris and there the new king was received in a series of triumphant receptions. At that moment began the most popular reign of any monarch in French history.

Henri IV was welcomed because he brought peace; he was loved because he was down to earth, embraced for his love affairs, and endorsed for wanting every peasant to have "a chicken in the pot" on Sunday. During his reign, cut short by his assassination in 1610 at the hand of a fanatical Jesuit, Paris became Paris. And also during his reign, the beautification of Paris, the remodeling of this city as a living symbol of the French state, first became a priority of the monarchy— starting a tradition that has continued, despite all the changes in governments, up through our own time.

HÔTEL DE LAMOIGNON (HISTORICAL LIBRARY OF THE CITY OF PARIS)

Paris became Paris. The Louvre was being rebuilt in the Renaissance style, but it was hardly a model for the world; that distinction would await the construction of the palace at Versailles. Under Henri IV, the Pont Neuf was completed; the place Dauphine was built adjacent to it on the Ile de la Cité; the place Royale was constructed near the Bastille, close by the site of the ill-fated Hôtel des Tournelles. Henri IV's chief minister, the duc de Sully, built a mansion on rue Saint-Antoine whose garden could be entered from the new place Royale. And there were more new mansions built in the Marais. But none of these could begin to rival, either in magnificence or architectural distinction, the palaces and squares that had been built in the previous century in Rome, nor those that were yet to be constructed there by the reigning genius of the age, Bernini.

No, what was unique to Paris was neither its architecture nor its urbanism. Instead it was the fact that it was the capital of the largest

nation of Europe, with both the court and the state officials in residence, and that it had become the social capital for all of France. This
is why there were more and more commodious town houses being built
in the Marais. And it was this confluence of wealth, culture, and political power that began bringing about the heady interaction of politics,
law, science, culture, and finance that was to give Parisian life its special
excitement and that would make all the other cities of France seem
"provincial" by comparison.

The reign of Henri IV was at the beginning of the seventeenth century, still called *le Grand Siècle* in France because it was the century during which that country became the model for all the other nations of
Europe, nations that had previously looked to Italy for what was up-to-
date. The seventeenth century saw the creation of the classic French
style in almost every field of human endeavor: art, literature, drama,
architecture, government, law, military strategy, even cooking. And it
was the great century for the Marais as well, the period during which
the Marais was the most fashionable neighborhood in Paris. So before
going further, let us take a look at the city when the house at the corner
of rue des Rosiers was already more than three hundred years old.

⚘   ⚘   ⚘

We begin with a bird's eye view. From high above, most of what we see
is a great bowl of wheat fields, with forests here and there, the fields
green in the spring, golden in the summer, with a bright meandering
river descending in wide curves from east to west. The woolly clouds
of the Ile de France drift overhead; below, in the countryside, there is a
sprinkling of villages, each with its modest church spire.

At the center of the panorama, however, there is a tight oval of tiled
roofs surrounding a small island in the Seine, a city with a total area
of no more than two square miles. Although there are monasteries
and villages not very far away, the shape of the city is perfectly clear; a

clear demarcation shows where the city ends and the country takes over.

Under those roofs and in the narrow streets that separate them, more than 400,000 people are living and dying, making this the most populated city in Europe. London covers a larger area, but in Paris people are packed more tightly together. The French have been used to living in apartments for centuries; it is only the very wealthy, in the new mansions of the Marais, who can afford to have a house of their own with a courtyard in front and a garden in the rear.

As we move in closer a few individual features stand out. There are five bridges linking the Ile de la Cité with the Right Bank and the Left Bank, all of them (aside from the Pont Neuf, which had been planned as a public esplanade from the start) crowded with houses. There are two forts, the Bastille to the east, on the Right Bank, and the Tour de Nesle on the Left Bank near the Pont Neuf. There are the massive new

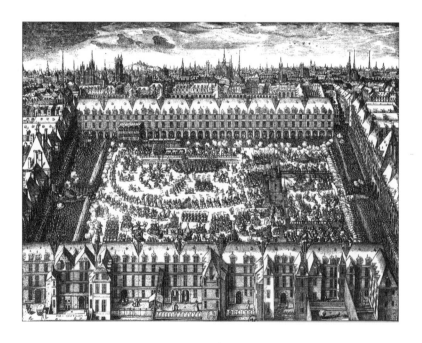

INAUGURATION OF THE PLACE ROYALE, 1612

buildings of the Louvre along the Seine to the west. But for the most part what rises above the sea of tiled roofs are church buildings: Notre Dame, the Sainte Chapelle, Saint Gervais, Saint Etienne du Mont, and so on. This is a city still dominated by church towers in the Gothic style, to which Parisians remain attached, perhaps because they created it. (Saint Eustache, that great barn of a church, all flamboyant Gothic, is entirely sixteenth century, contemporary with Saint Peter's in Rome.)

Of course a bird's-eye view of the city was an exercise of the imagination for people of the time, but by scaling the heights of Montmartre they could at least get an idea of its appearance from above. Indeed, that is the vision represented by most maps of the period, although these are usually drawn looking east from an imaginary point in the sky, so that the church fronts, which face west, could be shown.

To take a look at our corner in the Marais we have to go down to street level. And there we find that the house at the corner of rue des Rosiers still looks much the same as when it was built. It is still, legally, three houses, sharing a common foundation and cellars: one on rue des Rosiers, one at the corner, and one on rue Vieille-du-Temple. There are new houses on the north side of the street, but they look very much like the ones built three hundred fifty years earlier. The immediate neighborhood is still very middle class. The house (or three houses) at the corner has had a succession of different owners and inhabitants during the three hundred fifty years since it was built, some of their names recorded in documents that still exist. For example:

> 1393: the house* (rue des Rosiers) "at the sign of St. Julien" belonged to Robin Pasquier. (Corner house): This house belonged to Hennart de Cambenart, guardian of arms for the King. (Vieille-du-Temple): this house belonged to the above.
> 1410: (Vieille-du-Temple): sold to Giles de la Motte, wine merchant to the king.

* Here I am quoting from the study by Cournaud, op. cit.

1512: (Vieille-du-Temple): Gérard Lelièvre, a mason, bought it.

1560: (rue des Rosiers): Anne du Valle rented the house to Jérôme de la Veilleville, a lawyer.

1576: (rue des Rosiers): the widow of François Patard, silversmith for the Princess de la Roche, was living there.

December 12, 1598: a judgment in favor of Cyprien Proust for the possession of two houses, one on rue des Rosiers and the other on rue Vieille-du-Temple.

During those years, the roof must have been redone many times—roofs do not last for centuries—but by and large the structure remained largely unchanged. There were no pipes to leak or clog up, no wiring to dry out, no central heating to break down, no elevator to be replaced, no gas lines, no telephone connections, no TV antenna. A modern house is an elaborate machine for living: a medieval house was much more simple.

Indeed, if one of the original inhabitants of the house had returned three hundred fifty years later, he would have found his immediate surroundings reassuringly familiar. The speech of his neighbors would be hard to understand at first, with many new words and the pronunciation of the old ones distorted, as if the men and women of this new age were all talking through their noses. But after a few days the time traveler would have gotten the hang of that. If he had been a weaver, his old skills would still be valuable, the method of making cloth having changed very little. The food, on the other hand, if he were invited to any repast more elaborate than the simple supper of a working man, would likely taste overly salted and sweet, and in addition flavored with strange new spices from the Indies. He might be served some new varieties of fruit, such as raisins from Malta or even an orange. He would be surprised that so many people knew how to read and that what they read were books made of paper and that much of what they read was written in French instead of Latin. But all in all everyday life would seem much the same, regulated as before by the bells of the convent of

"…Saint Eustache, that great barn of a church…"

the Blancs Manteaux just across the street, the bells of Saint Gervais down by the Seine, and the deep *bourdon* of Notre Dame floating over the tight-packed roofs of Paris from the central island from which the city had first arisen.

Fortunately, we do not have to rely solely on our imagination to get a picture of our ordinary house in the seventeenth century. There are documents—about which, more later—that describe it in some detail. In these documents, the three houses are described as follows. The corner house: "a shop that opens on rue des Rosiers and on Vieille rue du Temple* with a kitchen behind, three rooms above with closets, attics above these, commodities, and all covered with tiles." In another place: "cellar, shop, kitchen, several rooms and attics above." The house next door on rue des Rosiers: "cellars, two rooms, attic above, commodities, a little court." And the third house, the one on rue Vieille-du-Temple: "a shop, cellar below, two rooms and closets along with them, an attic, a little court, all covered with tiles."

The same documents also tell us that the house at the corner was occupied by the family of a pastry maker, Etienne de la Porte, whose title was *paticier du Roi*. De la Porte had his shop at the corner on the ground floor with its fireplace and all-important oven behind. Next door, on rue Vieille-du-Temple, there lived Henri Bruslé, a grocer; his shop, identified as being "at the sign of the Caldron," was on the ground floor. The house facing rue des Rosiers had no shop on the ground floor and it was only two stories high. The house at the corner was four stories high—three above the shop—and over the grocery shop there were two stories. The court was shared by the two houses not on the corner and had a well. The house on the corner had its own well in the cellar.

---

* In all documents before the Revolution the street is named "Vieille rue du Temple" (Old Temple Street) to emphasize the distinction between it and the "rue du Temple." Then some bureaucrat (probably) decided that all street names must begin with *"rue"* and it's been "rue Vieille-du-Temple" ever since.

If, by the seventeenth century, the structures themselves were already old-fashioned with their narrow staircases and their half-timbered facades, their interiors would be just like those of the other, more recent dwellings up and down the street. There are no documents that specifically describe the furnishings of the apartments in the three houses at the corner, but there are so many inventories made after the decease of people of modest means at that time that we can be confident of knowing, in general terms, what a Parisian home contained.

If we could walk through those rooms today our first impression would be one of stuffiness and overcrowding—inexpensive but heavy tapestries covering most of the walls, heavy curtains covering the windows, with the principal pieces of furniture in most rooms some kind of oversized bed, most of them four-posters, again with heavy curtains. The largest of these beds were imposing structures and usually the most expensive furniture in any household; they consisted of a *paillasse* (straw mattress), covered by a *sommier* (horse-hair mattress, or something like it), then two or three *matelas* (presumably lighter, softer bedding), followed by sheets, blankets, and quilts. At the head were bolsters and pillows, and the whole structure had curtains about it. Stretched over the top was a piece of cloth called a *ciel* (literally, a "sky"). Such beds were often wide enough for several persons, but in addition there might be cots, folding beds and day beds with raised heads.

There were two reasons for all these curtains and beds. Most middle class apartments were overcrowded by modern standards, which accounts for the number of beds—the curtains created a certain privacy—but more important was the necessity of conserving heat. In Western Europe the years 1620 to about 1653 were what has been called a "little Ice Age," with freezing winters and cold, damp summers. Not every room had a fireplace and firewood was expensive, so in summer as in winter everyone wore heavy clothes and rooms and beds became domestic cocoons.

Still, every apartment had its fireplace, but it was usually only on the second story that the fireplace would be large enough for elaborate cooking. It would then be equipped in a way familiar to anyone who has ever visited an old country house in America or Europe, with iron pots, devices for hanging them over the logs at various heights, perhaps a spit for small roasts, perhaps a grill, also some kind of screen put before the fireplace when it was not in use to keep out drafts. The smaller hearths in the upper apartments, if not fully equipped, were surely used for simple cooking. Each apartment would also have a good-sized metal tank for water with a spigot so that it could be drawn a cup at a time. Remember that all water had to be carried up, either from a well for those living in houses fortunate enough to have one or from a public fountain in the street that might be several blocks away. Nowhere was much water wasted on washing.

No apartment had an oven; these were to be found only at bakers' or pastry makers'. For special occasions a middle class housewife might prepare a stuffed fowl and bring it to the bakery to be roasted—a custom that was still found in Paris as late as the 1950s—but for the most part even well-to-do people bought much of their roasted food from pastry makers, which explains the prosperity of that *"corporation"* (guild) whose numbers were limited by custom and decree.

In addition to the beds and curtains, the furniture would consist of wooden tables, stools, chairs, and wardrobes, which occasionally were built into the thick walls, like closets, consisting of wooden shelves behind heavy wooden doors. Aside from these essentials, we might find candlesticks, small mirrors in dark wood frames, a few books (probably pious works), perhaps a crucifix, perhaps a painting or two—biblical scenes or images of saints, family portraits or more rarely landscapes or still lifes. The ceiling would be held up by heavy wooden rafters or rows of narrow beams that were generally painted, either brown or dark red, or perhaps decorated with cartouches, florets, arabesques. The shutters at the windows were painted dark grey or brown. In this crowded interior all the colors were earthy or faded, with accents of dark green or blue or a fashionable pink: *"couleur de rose sèche."* If we could take a Polaroid photograph of one of these rooms, it would call to mind not so much a French painting of the period as a Flemish or Dutch interior—only in the Low Countries was the depiction of middle-class life considered a fitting subject for Art.

To return to the practical side of life, the documents mention *"aisances."* These would consist of wooden boards pierced with one, two, or three openings, placed either in a privy in the court or in closets off the staircase. Ceramic pipes below led to an underground tank that had to be periodically cleaned. Laundry was sent out to be done by washerwomen. We must remember that at this period there was no technological difference between life in a small village and in a great city; only different social arrangements necessitated by so many people being crowded together and living on top of each other. In many ways, city life was much less comfortable.

In all this, there is still nothing to bewilder our imaginary time traveler. But this apparent similarity of the way of living in this corner of Paris in the seventeenth century to what it had been three hundred fifty years earlier when the house was built is deceptive. In our own time we are so accustomed to daily life being transformed every generation by technological innovations that we regard such innovations as the prime indicator of historical change. In fact, there had been some important technological transformations in those three and a half centuries, even if they were not immediately visible at the corner of rue des Rosiers and rue Vieille-du-Temple. The printing press was one, which accounted for all those books and made possible all that literacy and had already created a *gazette* (from *gazzetta,* an Italian coin of little value), the beginning of what we call the press. Another was the enormous improvement of the capabilities of ocean-going sailing ships, which was responsible for the new foods on Parisian tables. Another was the substitution of guns and cannons for the pikes and arrows of the Middle Ages as the primary tools of warfare, which gave the monarchies of

Europe a decisive edge over the feudal barons who had contested their power in the past.

But the most profound transformations had been political and social. Primary among these was that Paris was now definitively the capital of one of the great powers of Europe, indeed of the greatest of these powers, as would be confirmed in the course of the century. As a result, there were to be no more walls around the city. The next time a hostile army occupied Paris would be in 1814, after the fall of Napoleon.

Linked to this was the radical transformation that religion brought about in the lives of ordinary people. Whatever it had been during the Middle Ages, and whatever passions had been aroused during the wars of the sixteenth century, religion had now become simply part of the established order, inspiring neither fervor nor skepticism for most people. It was there, part of the inherited furniture of daily life, even if the quarrels between Jansenists, Jesuits, and Freethinkers could inspire much debate among the intellectual elite.

The other transformation was that this society had become intensely legalistic. Maybe the printing press had something to do with it, having encouraged the spread of literacy, but the legal documents of the seventeenth century are practically all written by hand. Every profession had its *"corporation"*; every real estate transaction, every inheritance generated an enormous quantity of documents. There were over a hundred notaries in Paris alone. Paris had become a city of lawyers, and the *Noblesse de Robe* was one of the most wealthy and powerful groups in French society.

And, as might be predicted, France had become a society in which almost everyone was trying to acquire as much wealth as possible. French society was not yet what we call "capitalistic"—that would occur only with the Revolution. Theoretically the medieval "feudal" network of relations based on titles and obligations remained in force, but in practice it was wealth that conferred power. Not naked wealth, but rather wealth clothed in aristocratic trappings. A primary source of

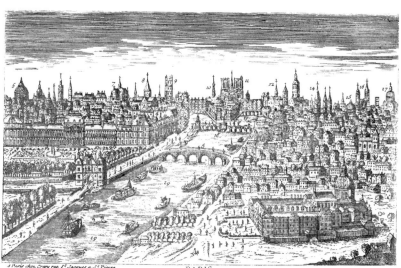

A SEVENTEENTH-CENTURY VIEW OF PARIS,
LOOKING EAST FROM LES INVALIDES (LOWER RIGHT)
TOWARD NOTRE DAME (CENTER)

the monarchy's power had always been its ability to bestow titles on wealthy individuals, titles that could be handed down and that would confirm the family's position in society, in return for a cash contribution. And also to award posts, both in the Church and in the State bureaucracy, that brought wealth to those appointed, who might often be the younger sons of titled families who needed an income.

If all of this sounds complicated, it is because it *was* complicated, so convoluted that at times it seems a deliberate mystification. New substance in old forms: that was the method of what after the Revolution was called the "Ancien Régime."

All of this has diverted us from the house on the corner of rue des Rosiers. But before returning, we should take a closer look at some of the house's more recent neighbors, the great mansions that became in this period the outstanding feature of the neighborhood that people were just beginning to call the Marais. One close by was the Hôtel d'Effiat, just a short way down rue Vieille-du-Temple, a great house in the grand style. We can't visit it any more, since it was torn down in 1882 to make way for the rue du Trésor, a short, dead-end street surrounded by solid but ordinary middle-class apartment houses. But when we do enter the remaining great houses of this period, many of which now serve as museums—the Hôtel Carnavalet (Museum of the City of Paris), the Hôtel Salé (Picasso Museum), the Hôtel de Donon (Jacquemart-André Museum)—all is clean and neat.

That was not the case when these great houses were built, serving as the beehive of activity that a residence of a great noble or government official required in those times. The rooms now are perfectly suited for a museum, but notice how one room leads into another and how there are no corridors permitting you to get to the room at the end without passing through all those in between. And yet there was a horde of family members, dependents, employees, servants who lived in those rooms, crowded together, sleeping in the same big beds surrounded by canopies and hangings that were found in middle-class houses. If you look for rest rooms in the modern museum you will find them, but there were none at the time they were built. Bathrooms, corridors, privacy— all that we take for granted as necessary in even the most modest dwelling—did not become part of the architectural vocabulary until a century later.

Instead, in those great houses, there was a constant press of people, coming in, going out, talking, scheming, and relieving their bladders almost everywhere, both the men and the women. Any corner would do, although fastidious men, such as the Cardinal Richelieu, were known to prefer the fireplace. The same behavior was found in the Royal Palace, the Louvre, and later in the century at Versailles. Strong smells were so much a part of the way of life of the time that almost no one noticed. Perfumes and aromatic herbs were sometimes burnt to camouflage the stench, but people were accustomed to living surrounded by filth; the streets, after all, were much worse.

Of course these great houses did have great rooms set aside for fêtes, galas, receptions, balls. Those rooms never had any beds. And the celebrations were frequent since they were the ultimate purpose of a great house. The ballroom would be lit by innumerable candles; the carriages would arrive in the courtyard; the guests would mount the wide staircase in the Italian style, made for show; musicians would play; footmen in livery would be in attendance.

And at some time there might be a pastry maker, such as one Etienne de la Porte, who might wheel out a huge ham covered with a sculpture of golden dough. This would have been a re-creation of the "masterpiece" that had been his test piece for being admitted to the guild of the *"paticiers du roi,"* a title that he had attained only after years of being an apprentice to his father-in-law, Claude Bourgeois, who had been for many years a Master pastry maker himself.

The profession of Claude Bourgeois and Etienne de la Porte was old and honorable. Its origins went back to the Middle Ages, when the house had been built. The pastry-maker's guild dated from the middle of the sixteenth century. Many of its rules, as well as the regulations of the City of Paris, were designed to maintain strict control over the quality of the goods being sold to the public. A good part of the business was the sale of meat pies, fresh cooked and steaming, but of unverifiable contents—especially since they were highly spiced—so there was a good reason for the regulations. As a result of the guild monopoly, the number of shops was limited and the prices of the meat pies higher than they would otherwise have been, but the customers were presumably protected. And the pastry makers, those who had earned the right to keep a shop, made a very good living.

Paticiers were part of a large middle stratum of those people referred to as *"bourgeois de Paris,"* who had the right to the title of "Master" of their craft, trade, or profession. In theory all those professions were open to apprentices who would learn their job by working for a Master. In practice, the title was usually passed from father to son, or to someone who married the daughter of a Master. This was precisely the case of Etienne de la Porte. His wife, Jacqueline, was the daughter of Claude Bourgeois, the *maître paticier,* who at the beginning of the seventeenth century owned the house at the corner of rue des Rosiers and had his pastry shop on the ground floor.

Claude Bourgeois died in 1640 and his son-in-law continued the business at the same location. But as for the house, Etienne de la Porte did not simply inherit it on the death of his father-in-law, as one might expect. He did eventually become its owner, but only at the end of a long legal process that resulted in the house being sold at a public auction. And this legal process is described in some notarial documents that have, fortunately and fortuitously, survived. Incomplete as these documents are, they provide important information about life at this street corner of Paris in the middle of the *Grand Siècle*—and they deserve a chapter of their own.

An Auction

"For arrears of the *rente* of two hundred *livres* due by the heirs of Claude Bourgeois, the aforesaid Champaigne having received nothing and having duly seized all the real property of the estate of said Bourgeois to obtain payment, which arrears due by the succession to the father in the sum of seventy seven *livres* one *sol* and four *deniers* being half of one hundred fifty-four *livres* three *sols* four *deniers* for nine months and eight days of arrears incurred since the twenty-fourth of March Sixteen Forty up to the following December. For the record."

—*Mémoire* of Philippe de Champaigne, 16 December 1642

WHEN THE HOUSE at the corner of rue des Rosiers was built, back in the thirteenth century, the land on which it stood was part of a *"fief,"* known as the *"fief d'Autonne."* Autonne may have been the name of a noble family that had been granted a parcel of land on the outskirts of Paris. The Middle Ages, as everyone knows, was the era of "Feudalism," which was a way of organizing the control of land by defining rights and obligations between individuals, rather than by ownership as we understand it today. It was a system already many centuries old by the time the house was built, and it had evolved as a response to the chaos that had followed the collapse of the Roman Empire. And indeed, the *fief d'Autonne* may well have been a farm or a vineyard some time in the past, the period that used to be called the Dark Ages.

The basic principle of Feudalism was military protection in return for agricultural labor, a kind of share-cropping in a barter economy. If the *fief d'Autonne* had originally been a farm, the people who actually worked the land would have been serfs, and much of the meager harvests they produced would have gone to people of higher status, perhaps Autonne himself, who was probably (as was the case with most nobles of the period) an illiterate warrior. But by the time the house was built, all of that was already long in the past. Probably by then the heirs of Autonne were already receiving money from the people who had built houses on what had been the family farm (assuming it had remained in the same family), a kind of ground rent known as the *cens*.

As it happens, the *fief d'Autonne* still exists on a modern map of Paris, since its limits coincide with what we call a "block," a word for which there is no French equivalent. This block is the area bounded by rue Vieille-du-Temple, rue des Rosiers, rue des Ecouffes, and rue du Roi-de-Sicile. Its history is better documented than that of most of the Parisian fiefs. If it had originally belonged to a noble family, by the fourteenth century it belonged to a bourgeois family whose name was Cocatrix. And on October 25, 1374, it was sold by Bernard Cocatrix to Etienne Porcher, sergeant-at-arms to the King. At that date the annual ground rent for all the houses that had been built in the previous century was probably still a substantial sum, so that the men who bought the houses from time to time had to take this *cens* into account to decide whether or not, as owners, they could make a profit in renting out the shops and rooms and apartments inside.

As early as the fourteenth century, then, the annual ground rent was being paid by one *"bourgeois de Paris"* to another. But this was Paris, not the country, and in cities an economy based on currency was already in place, even if Feudal forms such as *fiefs* remained in use. The term repeated in all the documents, *"fief tenu en franc alleu du Roi,"* may imply that the right to this fief comes directly from the King rather than passing through a noble intermediary. In the Middle Ages, the term "bourgeois," as in *"bourgeois de Paris,"* referred to a status rather than to an economic class and even less to a life-style. So it was not self-contradictory for a *bourgeois de Paris* to be the *seigneur* (lord) of a fief from which he collected the *cens*. And indeed in English, even today, the owner of a building who collects rent is called a "land-lord."

These payments were probably substantial when the house was built, worth far more than whatever share of the harvest of the farm or vineyard the Autonne family had received earlier. But they were fixed, once and forever. The feudal system, originally based on barter and share-cropping, made no allowance for inflation. The *cens* was fixed, for the three houses at the corner of rue des Rosiers and rue Vieille-du-Temple, at *"II sols, X deniers"* (in English terms: two shillings, ten pence). As the years went by, the successive owners of the house were able to raise the rents of their tenants to whatever the traffic could bear, but the *cens* remained fixed. And by the seventeenth century, when Etienne de la Porte had his pastry shop at that corner, that annual payment was a trivial amount, perhaps just enough to buy a couple of his meat pies.

Nonetheless, the owners of the houses continued to pay those feudal duties and for a very good reason: being in order and current on the records of the Lord of the fief was the equivalent of having a deed to the property. For the same reason, whenever a house was sold or mortgaged or inherited, a copy of all the documents was filed with that *seigneur*. But the business of being the Lord of a fief was probably becoming more trouble than it was worth. In 1673, title to the *fief d'Autonne* was transferred to the Hôtel-Dieu, the ancient main hospital of the city of Paris. My guess is that this would have been a charitable donation rather than a sale. One way or another, all the records of the *fief d'Autonne* were moved to the archives of the Hôtel-Dieu. And the houses' various owners now paid the annual ground rent to the hospital—among them Etienne de la Porte, who appeared on the 18th of August 1673 before noon and promised to make the same payment every year "on the day of Saint Rémy" for as long as he remained owner of the house—which he also promised to keep in good condition, so that the *cens* would always be paid if the house were rented.

Then came the Revolution, at the end of the eighteenth century. Along with other feudal institutions, all this legal medieval clutter of *fiefs* and *cens* was swept away. A *cadastre* was established for all the real estate of Paris (which was officially the *Département* of the Seine), listing and describing every single parcel of land and its owner. Any disputes, liens, or encumbrances on absolute ownership in the modern capitalist sense of ownership were null and void if they were not recorded in the *cadastre*. The *fief d'Autonne* no longer had any existence or real meaning, aside from memories.

As for the Hôtel-Dieu, it was in effect nationalized, which is to say it was henceforth run by the government. In fact, the institution is still functioning, almost exactly where it has been since the Middle Ages, on the Ile de la Cité facing the square in front of Notre Dame, but on the north instead of the south side. The current buildings are nineteenth century, not at all distinguished from an architectural point of view, and have been renovated inside to make the Hôtel-Dieu a modern municipal hospital, with nothing of the Middle Ages remaining aside from the name and the basic location.

After the Revolution, many of the archives of the pre-revolutionary institutions that had been nationalized were moved to the Hôtel de Ville, the Paris city hall, among them the archives of the Hôtel-Dieu, including all the papers concerning the *fief d'Autonne*. In the middle of the nineteenth century, these archives were catalogued, which is to say ordered in a logical fashion with a number assigned to each one; the result, with dates and a brief summary of the contents of each document, were published in a series of handsome volumes during the reign of Napoleon III. This was fortunate, for during the Commune at the end of the siege of Paris (1871), the insurrectionists set the Hôtel de Ville on fire. Many of the pre-Revolutionary documents stored there

THE HÔTEL-DIEU IN 1531
(FROM A NINETEENTH-CENTURY ENGRAVING)

were consumed by the flames; all that remained of many of the records were the catalogue notations.

The papers concerning the *fief d'Autonne*, however, survived. The Hôtel de Ville had been so badly burned that it was decided to tear it down and build a new one, and so the documents that had been saved had to be moved somewhere else. With a logic that was more bureaucratic than historical, the documents that had belonged to the Hôtel-Dieu were turned over to the Hospital Administration. Which is why the records of the *fief d'Autonne* are now in the Archives de l'Assistance Publique, housed at 9 rue des Minimes.

It was while turning the pages of the large, red-covered catalogue volume devoted to the *fief d'Autonne* that I first realized just how helpful the location of the house on rue des Rosiers was going to be. All the streets and alleys of Paris have always had names, but the numbering of houses began only in the eighteenth century. Previously houses were identified by the name of the owner, or a previous owner, or perhaps a shop sign or decorative detail—like the names of London pubs today. But the house at the corner was always described as *"une maison au coin de la rue des Rosiers et Vieille rue du Temple."*

However, a second, unanticipated problem arose when the old box containing the documents relating to the *fief d'Autonne* was brought out and I untied the ribbons and took out the file folders: I found that I could not read most of the papers I had in my hands. Some of the earliest documents were handsomely inscribed in large clear letters on vellum, but in medieval Latin. Those from later centuries were in a variety of hands, some of them obviously scrawled in haste, and often with notes and additions written in the margins, sometimes sideways. But almost all of the handwriting was illegible to me, aside from the numbers and certain names. Only when I got to the papers from the end of the seventeenth century could I begin to read what was written.

Ultimately, I overcame the obstacle of the handwriting by bringing copies of the documents to someone who was an expert in such matters and who could transcribe them for me. The language itself did not present a problem, French having changed very little in the past three hundred years. But what became clear, once I had read the documents and analyzed them, is that the story they had to tell was incomplete. They included the names of owners and a few tenants and some dates, but for the most part not much more than that.

Nonetheless, there were four documents relating a particular event concerning the house at the corner: its sale at public auction on January 10, 1647. What made these especially intriguing was that this sale, according to the catalogue, was instigated by Philippe de Champaigne, one of the major French painters of the seventeenth century. So that, for however briefly and peripherally, this ordinary house was associated with History, with a capital "H."

The house, or rather the three houses, were put up for sale because of the non-payment of a debt. Philippe de Champaigne had instigated the legal action that led to the auction, but it is apparent that the real cause of the sale was a falling-out among the heirs of Claude Bourgeois, the pastry maker who had originally owned all three houses. Shortly after the auction, the purchasers of the houses put records of the sale into the dossiers of the *fief d'Autonne* to validate their title. These included more than the details of the auction itself; they also contained descriptions of the property and excerpts of the legal actions

and judgments that had led to the auction. But they did not tell the whole story.

History is often a record of past disputes as told by the winners; we do not have a Carthaginian account of the Punic Wars. The same principle applies to what in French is called *"la petite histoire."* But even if incomplete, the documents do tell enough to permit some guesses as to what really happened at our corner in the Marais three and a half centuries ago.

❧ ❧ ❧

The first person we'll meet is Philippe de Champaigne, who was born in Brussels in 1602. He trained as a painter and while still very young showed such promise that the great Rubens tried to hire him as an assistant. (Like other successful artists of the time, Rubens had a stable of painters who lived and worked in his *atelier* in Antwerp; they did much of the actual painting of the acres of canvas commissioned by all the great families of Europe.) Philippe, however, decided instead to follow in the familiar footsteps of his peers: to go to Italy to study the paintings of the preceding two centuries. On the way, he stopped in Paris; he was then nineteen.

In Paris, the Queen Mother Marie de Médicis, the widow of Henri IV, had just finished building the Luxembourg Palace, her Italianate residence at the edge of the city on the Left Bank. To cover some of its walls, Marie had commissioned Rubens to paint the series of huge canvases depicting the life of her late husband in which she played such a prominent role—canvases that are now in the Louvre. If Philippe de Champaigne had gone to Antwerp he would have worked on them. It is possible that Philippe had a recommendation from the Flemish master to the Queen. One way or another, he was hired as assistant to the French painter Nicolas Duschene, who was in charge of the remainder of the interior decoration of the Luxembourg. In fact, Duschene gave

Philippe a room in his own town house on rue des Ecouffes, one of the streets that formed the boundary of the *fief d'Autonne*.

So instead of going on to Italy, Philippe stayed in Paris, working at the Luxembourg, painting landscapes and portraits to decorate the long series of rooms. There was, after all, more than enough work to keep him busy for years. During this time, Philippe fell in love with Duschene's daughter, Charlotte. In 1627, when he was twenty-five and she fifteen, the two were engaged.

Realizing that his future was in Paris, Philippe made a short trip to Brussels to wind up his affairs there and see his parents. On his return to France he found that Nicolas Duschene had suddenly died. Philippe married Charlotte as planned and also moved up to Duschene's post as director of the decoration of the Luxembourg. In 1629, he was naturalized as a French subject. So at the age of twenty-seven, he was an established painter with numerous apprentices working for him in his own studio. But that was not all that unusual for the period.

Two years later, the Cardinal Richelieu, chief advisor to the young king Louis XIII, forced Marie de Médicis into exile; she had to abandon the Luxembourg Palace, where she had been in residence for only four years. But Richelieu was too intelligent to dismiss the hard-working and talented Philippe de Champaigne. Instead, he employed him to decorate his own new residence, the Palais Cardinal, then at the western edge of Paris and now part of the complex of buildings called the Palais Royal. Later, Richelieu would commission Philippe to paint his official portrait in several versions, one of which today is in the Louvre and another in the National Gallery in London. This is invariably the image that comes to mind at the mention of the statesman who was the power behind the throne—that and the fictional character created by Alexandre Dumas in *The Three Musketeers*.

Indeed, Philippe de Champaigne, the perfect establishment painter, whose most daring action was to paint portraits of the nuns at the aristocratic but Jansenist convent of Port Royal, was to remain in favor for

PHILIPPE DE CHAMPAIGNE (SELF-PORTRAIT)

the rest of his life, whatever the winds of politics. One of the founders of the Académie de Peinture, he eventually died, highly honored, in 1674, during the reign of Louis XIV. His irreproachable and exemplary personal and family life may have contributed to this long and serene professional career.

Not long after the death of Charlotte's father, Nicolas Duschene, her mother, Marguerite Jacquet, remarried. Her second husband was a certain Claude Collin. Marguerite and Claude had a daughter, Louise Collin. During the same years Philippe de Champaigne and his wife had three children, two of whom died at an early age. But when in 1638, twelve years after Philippe's marriage, his wife Charlotte had died, Marguerite Jacquet had died, as had *her* second husband, Claude Collin, Philippe became the head of what remained of the Duschene family, namely his own daughter and various other descendants of his in-laws.

This was a responsibility he took very seriously, as evidenced by the numerous surviving documents relating to leases, purchases, debts, and lawsuits concerning family affairs in which Philippe was involved. But Philippe also had real estate transactions of his own, including the purchase of a house on the newly created Ile Saint-Louis, where he and his dependent family eventually moved, after the sale of the Duschene house on rue des Ecouffes.

These documents are so voluminous that they make you wonder when the celebrated Philippe de Champaigne found time to paint. Among them are several relating to the heirs of the *paticier* Claude Bourgeois, who owned the three houses at the corner of rue des Rosiers and rue Vieille-du-Temple.

Claude Bourgeois was married to Marie Lemaistre. (Incidentally, all the documents from this period refer to women by their maiden names. This is fortunate, since otherwise it would be impossible to figure out who was who.) At one point, before Philippe came to Paris from Brussels, Nicolas Duschene and Marguerite Jacquet had made a loan to Claude Bourgeois and Marie Lemaistre for an amount that, curiously enough, is never mentioned in the documents. Perhaps it was a kind of mortgage on the houses that Claude Bourgeois and Marie Lemaistre owned, though this is doubtful since it was not recorded in the records of the *fief d'Autonne*. So we don't know if the loan was secured by the house; we don't know the principal of the loan; and we don't know if the loan had a duration, and if it did, what it was. All we know is that the interest—the *"rente"*—was 200 *livres* per year. But that is sufficient to understand what took place later, at least from the legal point of view, since all that is ever mentioned in any of the papers is the unpaid *rente*.

When we turn to Claude Bourgeois and his heirs, things are much less clear than they are with the family Philippe de Champaigne inherited from Nicolas Duschene. But what is evident is a complicated family and a complicated family dispute. The adjective that comes to mind regarding this dispute and its resolution is "Balzacian," even though middle-class family disputes were not a subject for novels in seventeenth-century France, just as middle-class genre scenes were not yet a subject for art.

Claude Bourgeois and Marie Lemaistre had a daughter, Jacqueline, and a son, Guillaume. Jacqueline eventually married Etienne de la Porte, and it was Etienne and Jacqueline who inherited the family business, the pastry shop in the house at the corner. Etienne de la Porte had originally been a wine merchant, so he must have become a pastry maker after his marriage. As for Guillaume, he was born between 1617 and 1622.

Marie Lemaistre died at some time after Guillaume's birth. At that time a *tuteur* (guardian) was appointed to represent him legally, perhaps in connection with some property that Guillaume had inherited from her. The name of that *tuteur* was Gilles Duschene. Was Gilles Duschene related to Nicolas Duschene, the father-in-law of Philippe de Champaigne? Maybe and maybe not; the similarity of names may be pure coincidence. There are more questions of this sort to come later.

Claude Bourgeois had a brother, Louis, who also had the status of *maître paticier,* probably inherited, since he does not seem to have had his own pastry shop. Louis may have been the black sheep of the family—he was in prison at the time when Philippe de Champaigne brought his suit against the heirs of Claude Bourgeois. The evidence of this is that the summons demanding payment of the unpaid *rente* was delivered *"entre les deux guichets de prison Sainct Martin des Champs"* (perhaps a debtor's prison).

Gilles Duschene, the *tuteur* of Guillaume Bourgeois, was married to a woman named Marie Cortier. At some time before Philippe de Champaigne began his lawsuit, Gilles Duschene died. Etienne de la Porte then became the legal guardian of his wife's younger brother. And Marie Cortier, the widow of Gilles Duschene, then married Louis Bourgeois, the brother of Claude Bourgeois.

But Claude Bourgeois did not remain single for long after the death of his wife; he remarried. His second wife was named Magdelaine Cortier. Again there is nothing to prove it, but for the sake of the story let's assume that Magdelaine Cortier was the sister of Marie Cortier. It is not so rare for two brothers to marry two sisters. The dates and order of these deaths and marriages are not clear but the result is the same whatever they were.

Claude Bourgeois and Magdelaine Cortier had a child—unnamed in the papers—and then Claude Bourgeois died. After his death, the house at the corner and the one facing rue des Rosiers were inherited by Jacqueline Bourgeois and her husband Etienne de la Porte. The house facing rue Vieille-du-Temple seems to have gone to Louis Bourgeois and his wife Marie Cortier, at least for as long as Louis Bourgeois was alive. But the new owners didn't live there; that house was rented to the grocer Henri Bruslé, though whatever they received in rent was not enough to keep Louis Bourgeois out of jail.

As for Magdelaine Cortier, the second wife of Claude Bourgeois, she seems not to have had title to anything, although she is clearly one of the heirs of Claude Bourgeois. For this I have no explanation. But it would seem that she remarried just before the legal proceeding began, according to a note in the records of the Châtelet which mentions a *"contrat de mariage"* dated February 26, 1642, for the widow of Claude Bourgeois, *maître paticier*. This second husband was a surgeon living on the Left Bank, whose name was probably Charville.

We can now turn to the suit brought by Philippe de Champaigne. We don't know precisely when Claude Bourgeois died, but it was before September 7, 1639, when Philippe received a judgment from the Châtelet de Paris declaring that the heirs of Claude Bourgeois were responsible for the *rente* on the loan from Nicolas Duschene and Marguerite Jacquet to Claude Bourgeois and Marie Lemaistre—all of whom were then dead. At that date there was as yet no dispute—the interest had been paid regularly—and Philippe de Champaigne simply wanted to put in the record who was responsible for the payments.

The *rente* had been paid when due and apparently it was paid by someone through March 24, 1640. From what we know about the heirs of Claude Bourgeois we can assume that the payments had been made by Etienne de la Porte, even though the Châtelet had declared that *all* the heirs were responsible for the interest. But then the payments stopped and the legal clock began to tick.

At this point we can ask why Etienne de la Porte decided to stop making the payments. Did he foresee the ultimate outcome, that he would become the unchallenged owner of the house where he had his shop? That is doubtful. But it is possible that he had had enough of paying the *rente* for which all the others were also responsible. It would be only when Philippe de Champaigne threatened to have the three houses sold at public auction that Etienne de la Porte realized how he could profit from the sale of the houses; which is why he never resumed paying the *rente*.

The payments stopped and when two and a quarter years had gone by—which gets us up to June 24, 1642—the amount owed by the heirs of Claude Bourgeois was 450 *livres*. Philippe de Champaigne then filed papers to have the real estate owned by the heirs of Claude Bourgeois seized by the Court (the Châtelet) and sold at public auction to pay the debt, which is to say the three houses that became the ordinary house at the corner.

But in a society as legalistic as that of seventeenth-century Paris, so respectful of the rights to property that every child under the age of twenty-five needed a legal guardian if he owned anything of value, seizing real estate to sell at auction was a drastic action that took a long time. In fact, it took almost five years, since the auction at which the houses were sold occurred only on January 12, 1647.

During those years the debt continued to grow, so that by the time of the auction it would have been almost 1,400 *livres*. This is a healthy sum, but before asking what its modern equivalent would be, let's consider the fact that at the auction the three houses were sold for more than 25,000 *livres*. And that Etienne de la Porte, one of the heirs who refused to pay the *rente* during all that time, bought one of the houses, the one at the corner, for 11,600 *livres*. And that is a lot more than the 1,400 *livres* in unpaid *rente*. Clearly more was going on than at first meets the eye.

It is obvious that if all the heirs of Claude Bourgeois had felt it was in their interest to pool their resources and pay the 200 *livres* a year, they would have done so. And also that if Etienne de la Porte had felt it was in his interest to pay the 200 *livres* a year, *he* would have done so. So why didn't anyone pay the *rente*?

Jacqueline and Etienne were living in the house at the corner where their shop was located. Perhaps Guillaume, Jacqueline's brother, was living with them. But their title to the house—and also the one next door on rue des Rosiers—was not clear. We know it wasn't clear because the papers named all those other heirs as persons whose property would be seized if the *rente* wasn't paid—Louis Bourgeois and his wife Marie Cortier, Magdelaine Cortier, Magdelaine's minor child who may have received the name of her second husband, the surgeon Charville, and also the young Guillaume Bourgeois and the woman he later married, Marie Flache.

And during those five years, while the legal clock continued to tick, it is possible that Etienne de la Porte and his wife Jacqueline had become friendly with Henri Bruslé and his wife Marie, who lived and ran their grocery shop in the house next door on rue Vieille-du-Temple, the one Claude Bourgeois had left to his good-for-nothing brother Louis. Henri and Marie Bruslé had saved or perhaps inherited enough money to think of owning the house where they lived and worked. And they also knew about the *"saizé à la requête de Philippe de Champaigne."*

In any event, Etienne did not pay the *rente* and Jacqueline did not pay the *rente*, and if Guillaume had any other thoughts in the matter he couldn't do anything about it because Etienne was his legal guardian. And Louis Bourgeois, who was in prison, did not pay the *rente* and neither of the Cortier sisters paid the *rente*. And so the mills of justice ground inexorably on, the Châtelet sending out town criers *"par les quatre quatorzaines anciennes et accoustuméz,"* which is to say four times at two week intervals, always on Sunday as churchgoers came out from Mass, to announce that a certain property consisting of three houses at the corner of rue Vieille-du-Temple and rue des Rosiers was to be sold at public auction at the Châtelet at the request of Philippe de Champaigne, painter and *valet de chambre* to the King.

And the houses were sold.

The auction took place on Saturday, January 12, 1647. Present were about a dozen notaries, who were apparently the only persons permitted to place bids, each representing a different client. There was one notary who had a power of attorney for Jacqueline Bourgeois, one notary for Guillaume Bourgeois and his wife Marie Flache, one notary for Henri Bruslé, one notary for Magdelaine Cortier's child, one notary for Philippe de Champaigne, one notary representing Etienne de la Porte (although that was kept secret for the moment), and others representing outsiders. No representative for Marie Cortier, her husband Louis Bourgeois having died. As for the potential real purchasers, only Jacqueline Bourgeois and Henri Bruslé were present, their presence perhaps a prearranged show to conceal the fact that one of the notaries, Maître Hubert, was bidding for Etienne de la Porte, who had stayed home, perhaps making his meat pies as usual, assisted by his apprentice and brother-in-law Guillaume.

For the small house on rue des Rosiers, the least important of the three, the first bid was by Trudelle, the notary representing Henri Bruslé, for 3,000 *livres*. And after some other bids, Henri Bruslé took it, at 5,250 *livres*.

For the house on rue Vieille-du-Temple, where Henri Bruslé had his grocery shop "at the Sign of the Caldron," the bidding was begun by the notary Tardy, representing an unnamed client, at 6,050 *livres*. It ended with successive bids by Tardy and the notary Trudelle, representing Henri Bruslé, and ultimately Trudelle acquired it for Henri Bruslé at 9,175 *livres*.

For the house on the corner, the bidding began at 9,000 *livres* by the notary Mathurin, for an unnamed client. There were two other bids by notaries whose clients are not named, but the bidding ended in short order with Hubert, secretly representing Etienne de la Porte, taking it for 11,600 *livres*.

Five days later, on Thursday, January 17, 1647, Maître Hubert and Etienne de la Porte went to the Châtelet and declared that at the auction Hubert had been acting on behalf of Etienne de la Porte. Etienne de la Porte then signed the register of the auction, promising to pay all the debts that Hubert had acquired by buying the house at the corner and all expenses, interest, etc., that might be due.

Eight days later, on January 25, 1647, Henri Bruslé went to the Châtelet and paid into the court the sums for the two houses he had bought at the auction on January 12, noting that these were to be used to pay all outstanding debts on the two properties, including whatever might be owed to creditors of the late Claude Bourgeois, Marie Lemaistre, Louis Bourgeois, as well as Guillaume Bourgeois, the minor Charville, etc.—*including the unpaid* "rente" *and the principal due to Philippe de Champaigne.*

Thus the result of the auction was that the sums that Henri Bruslé paid for the little house on rue des Rosiers and the house on rue Vieille-du-Temple—a total of 14,425 pounds—paid all the debts of the heirs of Claude Bourgeois, including the interest and principal, whatever it was, of the loan from Nicolas Duschene to Claude Bourgeois and his wife. Philippe de Champaigne had obtained all he had demanded. As for Etienne de la Porte, he had "bought" the house at the corner for 11,600 *livres*, but since he was the principal heir of Claude Bourgeois, that was a fiction; he never bothered to pay that sum to the Châtelet.

Before the houses had been put up for sale, all three belonged to the heirs of Claude Bourgeois. Now two of the houses had been sold to Henri Bruslé and part of the proceeds had paid what was due to Philippe de Champaigne. By "buying" the house at the corner, Etienne de la Porte had established his clear and exclusive title to that one. As for any claims that other members of the Bourgeois family may have had, there is no record that they were ever paid anything; but if they were, it was not mentioned in the records of the *fief d'Autonne*. Title to the real estate had been wiped clear by the auction.

Since we don't know the amount of the principal of the loan on which the annual *rente* was 200 pounds, nor what other debts had to be paid off, we have no way of knowing the net amount Etienne de la Porte received from the money Henri Bruslé paid for the two houses he had bought. But it was probably a substantial amount. What did he do with it? We have no way of knowing, but there is the fact that today staircase A of the house at the corner—which serves the parcel that Etienne de la Porte purchased—rises two stories higher than staircase B, which is the access to the two parts that were sold to Henri Bruslé. And that the form of staircase B is medieval, while staircase A, although narrow, might date from the seventeenth century. So perhaps Etienne de la Porte decided to add a couple of stories on top of his house, with an attic above: two apartments to rent and a dry place to store flour. People did things like that in all the old neighborhoods of Paris in the prosperous years of the reign of Louis XIV, in the second half of the *"Grand Siècle."*

And then what happened? On November 25, 1660, Etienne de la Porte again promised to pay the ground rent to the *fief d'Autonne* for the house on the corner, which he owned free and clear because of the auction. And on August 18, 1673, he *again* promised to pay the ground rent, this time to the Hôtel-Dieu. And then? And then?

In the National Archives there is a paper, dated 1705, describing the house: "A first house, at the corner of said Vieille rue du Temple, belonging to the heirs of de la Porte, pastry maker to the king, occupied by Dubé, pastry maker, with as its sign an image of the Virgin." That is the last mention of de la Porte that I have been able to locate. The papers in the Public Assistance Archives have only two entries for the eighteenth century, one of them from 1787, which reads: "First house at the corner of Vieille rue du Temple, occupied by an official of the Lottery. Proprietors: Mlles Debray, rue de la Roquette, Faubourg St. Antoine, near the sign of the long bow." The house had become a rental property, with an office that sold lottery tickets and perhaps also pipe tobacco replacing the pastry. This is confirmed by a note in the margin of another document, to the effect that in 1792 the house belonged to *"les demoiselles* De Bray..." That was during the Revolution.

After that the records from the Hôtel-Dieu come to an end, as do all other such records. After the Revolution there were no more *fiefs* or *seigneurs* of building lots; real estate legally became private property, as it had in fact already been for centuries. The record is picked up in the Archives of the *Département* of the Seine, and it consists of lists of names of owners and tenants, with very little additional information.

The fact is that there is nothing more—or if there is I have not been able to find it. For Philippe de Champaigne there is a great store of documents available, although they contain no further information about the auction that he instigated, which was a minor matter so far as he was concerned. But for Etienne de la Porte or Henri Bruslé, nothing.

This will not be a surprise to anyone who has ever tried to prepare the family tree of an ordinary family, but it does tell us something about the nature and fragility of the past. We are not, after all, dealing with peasants or gypsies, nor with a society whose principal remains are shards of pottery. On the contrary, as we have seen, France in the seventeenth century was a society with a passion for putting everything down on paper in great detail. There were church records of baptisms, marriages and deaths. There were documents prepared by notaries for many important business transactions. When someone with any substantial property died—certainly anyone who owned a house—a notary would prepare a detailed inventory, including household effects and clothing. And then there were other records, like those of the *fief d'Autonne.*

So in the year 1700, to pick an arbitrary date, there probably existed a fairly complete written record of at least the outlines of the lives of Claude Bourgeois, Etienne de la Porte, and the rest of the family. But today, aside from whatever information may still exist in documents catalogued under other names, or not catalogued at all, there is only the story of the auction of the three houses in 1647.

... To the Present

THE WALL BUILT BY Philippe Auguste at the end of the twelfth century had been demolished by the early sixteenth century, permitting houses to be built on the north side of rue des Rosiers. The next wall out from the center, the wall erected by Charles V in 1470, remained standing for two hundred years, even though the city had been steadily expanding into the faubourgs on its far side. Then Louis XIV decided to tear it down and replace it with a series of streets twenty meters wide and embellished by rows of trees, a new form of urban space designated by the word that had originally meant the walkway on the top of a rampart, the "boulevard."*

This transformation of its perimeter radically changed the relation of the Marais to the rest of the city. Instead of being a dead end, the Marais now became part of the greater urban fabric, and in the process began to lose some of its identity and character. A generation later, in the early years of the eighteenth century, the winds of residential fashion shifted to the west; a new neighborhood, the Faubourg Saint-Germain on the Left Bank, became the desirable place to built palatial urban residences "between court and garden." The great houses of the Marais were by then considered old and old-fashioned, and were being divided into apartments.

But we must remember this was still the Old Regime; things

---

* From the Dutch *"bolwerc"* (bulwark).

changed but the pace was slow. Enough of the prestige of the Marais remained so that the first decade of the eighteenth century saw the construction of the two great houses of the family Soubise-Rohan, l'Hôtel de Soubise and l'Hôtel de Rohan-Strasbourg, the grandest of the grand mansions of the Marais, one facing rue des Francs-Bourgeois, the other rue Vieille-du-Temple, but joined together by a common garden.

By the end of the long reign of Louis XIV, the Marais had run out of space for new construction; the last of the remaining vegetable gardens had long since been reclaimed from the ancient swamps to become building plots. So these two new great houses were located back toward the city center, on land that had been built up since the Middle Ages. The occasion was the extinction of an ancient family that had been part of all the great moments of French history. This was the family of the Guises, whose medieval residence was on what is now rue des Archives and who owned a large block of buildings all around. So when all of this was put up for sale by the heirs, the Soubise-Rohan family snatched it up, not as an investment but as a construction site.

They did, however—and this is unique for the period—conserve a circular tower and a Gothic gateway of the old Guise residence, incorporating them into their classical new palace. No doubt this was motivated by a desire to remind the public that the Rohans also had links to a misty medieval past, but it was also an early instance of the Romantic sense of history that would flower a century later. So it is particularly apt that the Museum of French History should be located there today.

Although the Marais was replaced as the height of fashion by new neighborhoods to the west, it did not go out of style completely. Many families that had inherited its great houses continued to live there. But these were the more conservative and often the more bigoted elements of the aristocracy, so that by the last decades before the Revolution the Marais was synonymous with everything that was out of date and politically inert.

HÔTEL DE SOUBISE (MUSEUM OF FRENCH HISTORY)
"…the Soubise-Rohan family snatched it up…"

GATEWAY OF THE FORMER GUISE RESIDENCE,
RUE DES ARCHIVES
"...links to a misty medieval past..."

In his *Tableau de Paris,* published in 1782, Sébastien Mercier gave this description of the Marais:

Here you find yourself back in the age of Louis XIII, as much for habits as for outdated opinions. Next to the shining neighborhood of the Palais Royal, the Marais is like Vienna compared to London. What reigns there is not poverty but the full range of all the old prejudices: it is the refuge of families in decline. There you will find cranky, gloomy old men, opposed to any new idea, and opinionated old women who take issue with authors they've only heard about and never read: they condemn the *philosophes* as men *to be burned.* If you are unlucky enough to have supper there, you will meet only blockheads and will search in vain for an amiable man whose discourse expresses the brilliance of wit and the charm of sentiment; in such circles, such a man would mean one armchair too many and unbalance a salon. There you find antique furniture which seems to be imbued with ridiculous conventions and customs.

Even pretty women, if some evil star has relegated them to this sad neighborhood, dare invite no other guests than retired generals or judges. But the most curious thing is that all these dullards hate each other and bore each other to death. The light of the arts shines on them only from a great distance; reduced to the *Mercure de France* for their information, they know nothing else.

If it should happen that an intelligent man, wandering by chance through these tiresome circles, should strike a few sparks, you will see the company rouse itself from its torpor to sneer at the fire that has awakened it. But then someone takes out a deck of cards, and it will be a year before they learn that day's news.

I've rarely seen such cloistered houses where, for lack of any other amusement, the eternal occupation is to deal and re-deal a deck of cards during the brightest hours of the day and the finest seasons of the year.

Another observer, the painter Elisabeth Vigée-Lebrun, reported having seen a long rank of "old ladies of the Marais, seated gravely on chairs, their cheeks so painted with rouge that they looked exactly like dolls. Since at that time only women of high rank had the right to wear rouge, these ladies thought they must indulge in the privilege to its full extent. One of my friends who knew most of them reported that at home they did nothing but play lotto from morning 'till night. One day... some of them asked for the news of Versailles; he answered that M. de la Pérouse [the navigator] was about to leave on a voyage around the world. 'Really!' the lady of the house exclaimed. 'That must be someone who doesn't have anything else to do!'"

Even these iron-willed caricatures of the great aristocrats of the age of the Sun King were swept away in the whirlwind of the Revolution, along with the *fief d'Autonne* and so many other remnants of the past. The Marais was associated with none of the great events of the Revolution, aside from the taking of the Bastille at its very beginning. The extremist *sans-culottes* were recruited more often in the working class Faubourg Saint-Antoine, on the other side of the Bastille, than from the varied petit bourgeois of the Marais, such as the ones who must have lived at the corner of rue des Rosiers at the time; records mention a tobacconist and a violinist. But two of the sites of the Massacres of September 1792, when bands of vigilantes executed thousands of accused counter-revolutionaries in the prisons of Paris, were the Prison de La Force on rue Pavée, and especially the women's prison on rue du Roi-de-Sicile. And during the last six weeks of the Terror in 1794, the windows of the houses on rue Saint-Antoine, which had seen the crowd that stormed the Bastille in 1789, looked down on the frightening processions of *charettes* carrying thousands of "suspects" to the guillotine at the Barrière du Trône at the eastern edge of the city—suspects who included servant girls and children, arrested for an injudicious remark.

With the triumphs of Napoleon around 1800, the eclipse of the

THE PRISON DE LA FORCE IN 1855
(NOW DEMOLISHED)

Marais was complete; the luminaries and events of the Empire passed it by completely, aside from the building of a model neighborhood market a block up rue Vieille-du-Temple from rue des Rosiers on the site of a former convent, itself on the site of a sixteenth-century mansion, the Hôtel d'O. (On rue des Hospitalières Saint-Gervais, two curious sculptures of steers' heads in an almost Assyrian style still adorn the walls of what was originally the meat market.)

The Restoration did not restore the Marais. Instead it was taken over by small-scale industry, wholesale commerce, and cheap housing. The two remarkable eighteenth-century palaces built by the Soubise-Rohan family were saved when the government took them over to house the National Archives and the National Printing office. Other great buildings were saved because they were too big to tear down; but their interior spaces were now used for manufacturing or classrooms, their courts or gardens roofed over for repair shops or garages. Some of the old families still lived on in the Place des Vosges, which because of its trees and architecture was always considered a desirable piece of Parisian real estate, even if not exactly fashionable.

The Marais never became a slum; it was simply one of many old and

run-down Parisian neighborhoods with neglected vestiges of the past mixed in with modern commerce and housing. This is evident in the works of Balzac, who spent his youth in the Marais. Balzac completed his undergraduate studies in a school installed in part of the Hôtel Salé, now the Picasso Museum; he wrote his first work in a garret in the Marais, a five-act drama called *Cromwell* that everyone then and since agrees is a disaster; he lived there while studying law and writing his first novels, pot-boilers published under pseudonyms.

When he was twenty-five Balzac moved to the Left Bank, and later to Passy, then still a village outside of Paris. It is his residence there, where he wrote his first serious works, that is now the Balzac Museum. The Marais, the neighborhood of his early youth, provides the backdrop for many of the characters in his novels, but then so does every other part of Paris. In writing about the Marais, however, Balzac displays a knowledge of the neighborhood's history that was unusual at the time, a time when even its name was almost forgotten.

Sometimes, however, this knowledge is not strictly accurate. In *Honorine,* for example, Balzac describes a visit to "a mansion as vast as the Hôtel Carnavalet" that is clearly a fantasy, perhaps based on the Hôtel Soubise:

> A peristyle of a magnificence worthy of Versailles led to one of those staircases that are no longer constructed in France, taking as much space as a modern house. Mounting the stone steps, cold as a tomb, on which eight men could walk abreast, our steps echoed under sonorous vaults. One could be in a cathedral. The banisters offered miracles of finely worked iron, expressing the fantasy of an artist of the reign of Henri III. Gripped by a mantle of frost that fell on our shoulders, we crossed antechambers, salons leading from one to another, with uncarpeted parquet floors, furnished with those superb old pieces that are the delight of antique dealers. Finally we arrived at a grand office situated in a square pavilion whose windows opened on an immense garden.

This flight of the imagination aside, Balzac describes the Marais as a quiet backwater: "At midnight the Marais has already been asleep for three hours. Its main street, rue Saint-Louis [rue de Turenne], and its center, the Place Royale [Place des Vosges], are buried in shadows and slumber." Or, in *Cousin Pons,* one of Balzac's last and greatest novels, he paints rue de Normandie as "one of those streets where you could imagine you are in a provincial city; grass grows between the paving stones, a passer-by is an event and everybody knows everybody else."

We must remember that Balzac wrote before the titanic transformation of the city by Baron Haussmann and his successors in the second half of the nineteenth century. What is special about the Marais today is precisely that, for the most part, it was spared the radical surgery performed elsewhere. The creation of the Boulevard Saint-Germain on the Left Bank, cutting through the Faubourg Saint-Germain and the Latin Quarter, caused the destruction of as many palatial and historic buildings as exist in the Marais today. And afterward it took almost a century for this special character of the Marais to be recognized. During the first half of the twentieth century, the official plan for the Marais was the same modernization as had happened everywhere else.

It was during this period of official neglect that rue des Rosiers and the streets surrounding it became the *Pletzel* (little square), the neighborhood where Jewish immigrants from Eastern Europe recreated the life of the ghettos and *shtetels* they had left behind, with Yiddish as its *lingua franca*—just as, at very much the same time, the same type of neighborhood was created on the lower East Side of Manhattan.

Despite the fact that rue Ferdinand-Duval, which forms part of this district, had originally been called rue des Juifs, the creation of the *Pletzel* had nothing to with any medieval tradition. The center of Jewish life in Paris before the expulsion edict of 1394 had been several blocks to the west, around rue du Temple. After the Revolution, which brought with it religious freedom, the first official synagogues were built by Jews from Alsace and Lorraine, but again some distance away,

HÔTEL SALÉ (PICASSO MUSEUM)

near what is today the Ecole des Arts et Métiers. No, the Jews from Eastern Europe settled around rue des Rosiers simply because by then this corner in the Marais had become one of the poorest districts in Paris. All immigrant populations in the nineteenth century tended to cluster in distinct neighborhoods, and Jews perhaps more than others because of their need to be close to kosher butchers and restaurants.

And so between 1850 and the Second World War the *Pletzel* flourished, with all the intensity and variety that characterized Jewish communities everywhere. Jews were traditionally second-hand clothes dealers, hat makers, tailors, cabinet makers, furriers—the same type of occupations that had characterized this corner in the Marais since rue des Rosiers had been laid out. There were Jews who were intensely religious, others routinely religious, others atheists. There were Communists and Zionists, with all possible permutations. The community grew, spreading out past the limits of the Marais to Belleville. Certain families who prospered left the neighborhood and often Paris altogether, returning perhaps only at Passover to buy matzos.

Much of this came to an end during the Occupation in the 1940s, when the Stars of David on the doors of kosher butchers, bakeries and restaurants appeared along with the obligatory yellow appliqués on the clothing of the inhabitants. There were frequent raids, carried out by the French police, to round up Jews whose names appeared on the typewritten lists of individuals marked for "deportation." (Many of these lists are conserved today in the library of the Memorial to the Unknown Jewish Martyr on rue Geoffroy-l'Asnier, behind the Hôtel de Ville.) On July 16, 1942, during what is known as *"la rafle du Vél d'Hiver,"* it took the efforts of forty policemen to fill—mostly with children—the buses that had been waiting on rue de Rivoli since dawn.

In the years between the two World Wars, the former Napoleonic meat market on rue des Hospitalières Saint-Gervais had been converted into an elementary school, with a special schedule to accommodate the Jewish children who lived nearby—there were no classes on Saturday.

An inscription on its wall pays homage to the principal of the school who, during the Occupation, managed to save dozens of his students from being rounded up. Nonetheless, a second inscription, to the right of the Assyrian bull's heads, reads as follows:

> 165 Jewish children of this school
> Deported to Germany during the Second World War
> Were exterminated in Nazi concentration camps.
> Do not forget!

Between the Jews who had been deported and those who had moved away, the district was only a pale shadow of itself after the war. Then came the influx of Jews from North Africa, who revived, for several decades, the neighborhood's Jewish character, adding falafel and couscous to the more traditional gefilte fish and challah as local gastronomic specialties. But with the upgrading of the neighborhood, even rue des Rosiers now has more boutiques featuring the creations of young *couturiers* than kosher butchers. The traditional Turkish bath or *hammam* has now been replaced by a restaurant. It is uncertain how much longer the tourists looking for "the Jewish neighborhood" will have anything more ethnic to discover than Goldenberg's restaurant.

ෂ෯ා   ෂ෯ා   ෂ෯ා

The papers my wife and I received when we bought our apartment include the "Rules of Co-propriety," as well some information about previous owners going back to the beginning of the twentieth century. The first entry is familiar: in 1901 the building was acquired at an auction held by the Tribunal Civil de la Seine, following a *"saisie"* according to a judgment of 1896. The new owner was a Monsieur Henri P., who held the property until his death in 1931, when it was divided among his heirs. This division was formalized as what we would call a condominium in 1962. At the same time a number of the apartments were put up for sale.

In 1973 the four small lots constituting the sixth and seventh floors reached by staircase A—our apartment—were acquired by a Mme S. What follows is not documented, but is information I gathered by talking to certain of the people involved. Mme S., at that time, was the owner of the Chevaliers du Temple, a successful restaurant and jazz club occupying the entire street level and the *caves*. She had bought the two attic floors to house one of her employees, a Tunisian immigrant, who went to the Halles early every morning to buy supplies and who shut up the premises late every night, activities that made it convenient to have him lodged on the premises.

Of course, this was before the renovation, and the apartment then was nothing like what it is now. It consisted only of the space on the sixth floor, the seventh being a storage area reached by the trap door over the landing. There was no kitchen or bathroom; only a sink inside the apartment and a toilet at the top of the stairs. The sixth floor space was divided into three small rooms with a partition bisecting the large window facing rue Vieille-du-Temple. These three small rooms were home to the employee, his wife and two daughters, plus frequent guests, other recent immigrants, many of whom stayed for weeks.

It was a year or two before we bought our apartment that the Chevaliers du Temple went out of business. The restaurant and cellar space had been rented to the first of a series of owners who tried to repeat the success of the club. Mme S. had sold the lots on the sixth and seventh floors to a developer, who renovated the space to create our pied-à-terre. The Tunisian family found another place nearby and at the time we moved in they were still frequently in the building, since it was they who put the garbage can outside at night and cleaned the halls and stairways. Talking to them, I learned what the apartment had been before.

But ours was not the first renovation at this corner in the Marais, and it will certainly not be the last. Redoing an entire neighborhood is a long process, especially when it is as large as the Marais, and especially when it is done as a series of individual projects, some public, some corporate and some strictly private. In France, as much as anywhere, the thicket of rules, regulations, and permits to be hacked through for any construction or remodelling project is dense. This is especially true in an Historic District, which in addition to the usual regulations also has numerous requirements relating to esthetics and historical accuracy. The work starts and stops, then continues without any abrupt transformation of a street or corner, and by the time it is finished you have forgotten just how it looked previously.

The building directly across rue Vieille-du-Temple from our windows was an exception to this rule because it was new construction. There is a photograph of the end of rue des Rosiers that must have been taken in 1962, because there is a sign over the front door of our ordinary house advertising apartments for sale. On the far side of rue Vieille-du-Temple one can see part of a rundown two-story building with a sign advertising "Charcuterie du Passage." This "passage" was the nineteenth-century shortcut to rue des Guillemites through several archways and two courtyards known as the "Passage des Singes." It is mentioned by Victor Hugo as a notorious den of thieves, although in Atget's photos (such as the one in the first chapter of this book) it looks more like the set for a silent film, with innocuous vegetable and housewares shops.

But when we first moved in there was a gap in the line of buildings facing us where the building in the 1962 photograph had been torn down. There had certainly been another structure adjacent to it, because just up the street were two stories of a rococo facade, propped up with wooden stays like a set in a film studio. Construction on the site had actually begun some time before; the two lots had been excavated and a deep parking garage constructed, covered with a concrete roof from which projected stubby concrete columns with steel cables sprouting like metallic weeds. But for several years nothing happened and over the rooftops of the next street, rue des Guillemites, we had an anachronistic view of the metal ducts and steel girders of the Pompidou Center rising half a mile away at the edge of the Marais like a stranded space ship.

THE POMPIDOU CENTER SEEN FROM
RUE SIMON-LE-FRANC

But then one fall the work resumed and went fairly quickly. In the spring we received a letter from a friend who was staying in our apartment announcing, "I saw Beaubourg disappear before my eyes!" When we returned in July, we were face-to-face with a new "historic" building, incorporating the rococo facade but otherwise discreet, with a slate Mansard roof at our eye level and gabled windows through which we could see spacious rooms with terra cotta tiled floors. Beside the front door of this apartment building, someone had had the nerve to put up a blue street sign that read "Passage des Singes."

For a while this structure called attention to itself by its very newness. But then tenants moved in and put up curtains; and the rain, catching the dust and soot, painted streaks on the new stucco walls; and when we had guests who didn't know the neighborhood they were surprised to learn that the building across the street hadn't been there all along.

The completion of this new building across rue Vieille-du-Temple did not mean peace and quiet for us; in fact at no time since we moved in has there not been some noise of construction or repairs going on right at our corner. Looking out across rue des Rosiers, we used to see a stretch of wall with a sinister (or picturesque) crumbling appearance, part of the top floor of a large building that at the time housed the "Swing" bar, frequented by young people with unisex short and dyed hair. But then came that building's turn to be fixed up. A scaffold of metal pipes and wood planks was erected, then covered with plastic netting to contain the dust, and the work began.

The general verb for fixing up in French is *retaper*. It was particularly apt in this case, since the work consisted of chiseling away most of the old stucco—*tap-tap-tap*—often down to the crude masonry wall. The workmen, of whom we had a close-up view, took care to catch as much of the debris as possible in plastic sacks, which were then lowered by pulleys to the street below; then, eventually, they applied new stucco of the durable and handsome kind that is prescribed for the Marais. The job was done in a highly professional way; nonetheless, despite an unusual stretch of fine weather, it was weeks of *tap-tap-tap*.

But that was nothing compared with what we had experienced in our own apartment a year earlier. In addition to having to climb five flights of stairs, part of the price of the light that comes from living just under the roof is damage from leaks. There had been minor infiltrations from time to time, but complaints to the *"syndic"* produced only the answer that money to repair the roof had not yet been approved. Then one fall night, after a driving rainstorm, we found our bed completely soaked, along with most of our clothes. The next day the *"syndic"* sent someone to inspect the roof—no easy job since it involved climbing a ladder at the top of the stairs, crawling through a trap door, and then scrambling out a dormer window where the only footing was the rain-gutter.

The inspector returned shaking his head. There was no sense in trying to patch here and there; a whole new roof was needed. A tarpaulin coated with plastic was installed as temporary protection, covering our skylights. The *"syndic"* took bids from roofing contractors and one of these was approved at the annual meeting of the apartment owners. It turned out to be an expensive job for the area covered, which was only the roof over our apartment. The expense was partially due to the cost of putting up scaffolding and partially because, under the rules governing any work in the Marais, the tiles had to be an approved "historic" variety, which are very dear. Now, I am, I suppose, in favor of the concept of historic authenticity, but I have yet to find any place on a sidewalk or even the middle of a street from which it is possible to see our roof. I suspect that the only place from which it is visible is one of the apartments of the new building across rue Vieille-du-Temple. The tenants of that apartment often leave their windows wide open on warm days in the summer and they play lovely music on their stereo; they also sometimes watch *CBS News,* which is rebroadcast every morning at seven by Canal Plus, and sometimes I am awakened by the voice of Dan Rather. Whoever they are, I hope they enjoy their "historic" view of our roof.

The scaffolding they put up was a curious structure. It was cantilevered out from the landing outside our front door and braced with struts across rue des Rosiers, reaching through the trap door in the ceiling toward a dormer window that, since our apartment was remodeled, illuminates only a narrow crawl space. (This window was not included in our apartment precisely so it could serve as access to the roof.) From the street the structure had an almost medieval appearance, like a pro-jecting battlement. The construction materials—chiefly the roof tiles—were carried up by ropes and pulleys from the street below; thus the entire operation made no use of modern technology whatsoever.

Fortunately for us, we were away from Paris during most of the sev-eral months of the work. When it was finally completed and the sun could again enter through the skylights, we felt curiously liberated.

Neighbors

*I*F YOU TAKE rue Vieille-du-Temple from its beginning, walking up from rue de Rivoli, the first intersection on your right is rue du Trésor, which is actually a cul-de-sac. This is a street of late nineteenth-century middle-class apartment buildings that occupy the site of an ornate seventeenth-century mansion, the Hôtel d'Effiat, destroyed in 1882. A few steps further to your left is the beginning of rue Saint-Croix-de-la-Bretonnerie, whose name dates from medieval times. On the north corner there is the Hotel Central, the best known and most convivial gay bar in Paris. A few more steps brings you to the western end of rue des Rosiers, at whose corner is, of course, the house with our pied-à-terre.

Continuing up rue Vieille-du-Temple on the left sidewalk, you come to a large and brightly lit shop that specializes in fine teas and coffee and has been there for decades, as its out-of-date name "La Maison des Colonies" indicates. Just past the shop is a *porte cochère* that is almost always firmly closed by two massive oak doors, each decorated with an expressive and somewhat frightening head of Medusa—probably the most remarkable doors in all the Marais. If you cross the street to take a better look, taking care not to be run over by a motorcycle, you will notice that the stone wall above the shop and to either side of the doors is black with soot, the same blackness that used to

DOORWAY, HÔTEL DES AMBASSADEURS DE HOLLANDE
"...a frightening head of Medusa..."

characterize the entire city of Paris before the massive clean-up of the 1960s. From this you might deduce that the building belongs to an institution exempt from the municipal regulations covering periodic maintenance of building facades, and you would be right: the house belongs to a foundation devoted to helping aged and indigent artists.

Should you manage to open one of the oak doors, you will certainly be stopped by the guardian, who will inform you that you are on private property and have to leave. You will barely have time to catch a glimpse of the court with its sundials, lintels, carved masks, and an archway under the principal facade leading back to a second courtyard whose existence you can only divine. And that is all you will be able to see of this remarkable building, among the most famous of the Marais hôtels, the Hôtel des Ambassadeurs de Hollande.

In 1655, the financier Amelot de Bisseuil decided to remake three buildings that his father had bought some years before on a narrow lot that ran from rue Vieille-du-Temple to rue des Guillemites; he wanted an elegant residence for himself and his family. Bisseuil hired the architect Pierre Cottard to plan the transformation and a variety of painters to decorate the remodeled rooms. Despite a cramped site and rooms too small for a great house, what was created over a five-year period is one of the treasures of the Marais. Unfortunately, it is one that is known chiefly from photographs, since visits are only by appointment and difficult to arrange.

A few generations later, with the Marais remaining a good neighborhood but no longer as fashionable as it had been, the house was rented out. From 1720 to 1727 it was the residence of Marius Guitton, who was the chaplain of the Dutch Embassy. It is presumably from these seven years that the popular name of the house derives, "House of the Ambassadors of Holland."

This tenant was also the source of what may or may not be a legend about the house, that of the Protestant services held there. Since 1685, the date of the revocation of the Edict of Nantes, Protestants, Protestantism, and Protestant worship had been officially banned in France. The Dutch ambassador, however, was permitted to have private services in the extra-territorial seclusion of his Embassy; it was for this purpose that he had a Chaplain. And although it was strictly forbidden, the Dutch ambassador might stretch the rules a bit and invite prominent Huguenots and their wives to these services. Not all Huguenots, in fact, had left France; some had remained, secretly faithful to the religion of their fathers, while officially pretending to be Catholic converts.

The real Embassy was not the house in the Marais; it was on rue Saint-Honoré, in a more fashionable and modern neighborhood to the west. But the chapel on rue Saint-Honoré was small and, in the more tolerant atmosphere of the Regency that followed the death of the Sun

King (or so the story goes), more and more closet Protestants dared to risk being noticed visiting the Dutch Embassy of a Sunday morning. There were so many that the Embassy chapel became over-crowded. And so the chaplain, to oblige these friends of his employer, began to hold additional services in the remarkable town house he had rented on rue Vieille-du-Temple.

We can even speculate that this was the reason why the Chaplain had rented so large a house, which otherwise would seem too luxurious a residence for a man of God, however large his family. We may imagine the carriages clattering up on a wintry Sunday morning, probably very early, awakening the inhabitants of the neighborhood. And then the forbidding Medusa-head oak doors swinging open. And the simple hymns and homilies in the not-so-grand gallery of the central pavilion between the two small courts; the thin voices resounding under Michel Corneille's paintings on the vault, already half a century old: lots of bare flesh but plenty of cloth to preserve the modesty of his mythological figures, especially necessary since the point of view is from below. We can imagine the faithful at this quasi-clandestine service, dressed in clothes that are rich and black: rich because they have stayed in France to preserve the family fortune instead of emigrating to Berlin or the Delaware Valley, and black because it is the sign of just how serious they are about life and religion, which for them is one and the same... In fact we can imagine anything we want, since this is only a legend; there is no documentation that it ever happened.

Nobody remembers the subsequent tenants in the fifty years after the Dutch chaplain moved out. But then, in 1776, the house was occupied by a man who was the creator of a memorable character and himself a legend, Pierre Augustin Caron de Beaumarchais.

In English-speaking countries, Beaumarchais is known today chiefly as the author of the plays on which the libretti of *The Barber of Seville* and *The Marriage of Figaro* were based. But in France he belongs to literature and in his own time he was a unique phenomenon: playwright,

pamphleteer, man of letters, publisher, and also diplomat, spy, specula-
tor, and a molder of ideas. And on rue Vieille-du-Temple he would
assume a new role, that of what we would call today "gun-runner," or
perhaps "director of covert operations."

The year was 1776. The French, having recently lost the Seven Years
War against Britain and with it their colony, Canada, were following the
politics and protests of the thirteen North American colonies with great
interest. It was clear that war and even independence might eventually
result and that this would be in the interests of France. The Americans
were aware of this as well, and the envoy of Massachusetts in London,
Arthur Lee, had already begun to sound out the French government
about possible assistance in the case of war.

Louis XVI, however, did not want another war, at least not yet.
Beaumarchais, having conceived a great enthusiasm for the American
cause and its eventual benefits to France, sent off memo after memo to
the Foreign Minister, Vergennes, offering his services in any possible
capacity. In June 1776 he received a positive reply; Louis XVI was will-
ing to supply arms to the Americans so long as the operation was kept
secret. It was agreed that Beaumarchais would be in charge.

Beaumarchais immediately set up a trading corporation named
"Roderigue, Hortales & Cie." and rented the Hôtel des Ambassadeurs
de Hollande as the company's place of business. (It also became his residence.) Vergennes secretly gave him a million *livres* in cash to set the
operation going and promised that Spain, as France's closet ally, would
supply another million. After that, Beaumarchais's operation would
have to become self-supporting. The idea was that Beaumarchais would
buy ships and arms to give the Americans; in return they would send
Beaumarchais great quantities of indigo, which Beaumarchais would
then sell at a profit to buy more arms for America, and so on—all of
this in absolute secrecy. Note that this scheme was set in motion before
the Declaration of Independence. Returning from a trip to Bordeaux to
buy ships, Beaumarchais met the new American envoy to France, Silas

Deane. Deane, on behalf of the Americans, promised to pay any losses Roderigue, Hortales & Cie. might incur and told Beaumarchais that the immediate need was for 200 cannons, many mortars, 25,000 rifles, and tons of gunpowder.

Beaumarchais then bought a total of ten ships, spreading his purchases over six different ports for secrecy. He also persuaded the French War Minister, Saint-Germain, to give him 200 new army cannons, from which Beaumarchais had the French royal coat of arms removed. In August the Spanish came through with the promised additional million *livres* and the operation began, including the despatch of fifty "advisors" who accompanied the arms.

By 1777, the cost of the arms Beaumarchais had sent to America added up to five million *livres* and he had yet to receive any indigo in return. In March of that year Benjamin Franklin arrived in France where he was received by the King and Queen at Versailles and lionized in Paris as the great American philosopher. Of course his real mission was to convince King and country to enter the war officially. Meanwhile, Beaumarchais's covert operation continued. He persuaded Vergennes to give him another three million *livres*, but still the operation remained deeply in debt.

By the end of 1777, Franklin had persuaded Louis XVI to recognize the independence of the United States and to sign a treaty of alliance. In June 1778, France officially entered the war against Great Britain and Beaumarchais's covert operation was no longer necessary. By that time the government of the United States officially owed Beaumarchais more than ten million *livres*—a debt that remained on the books until 1835, when Congress finally voted to settle with Beaumarchais's heirs.

It was also in the Hôtel des Ambassadeurs de Hollande, on July 3, 1777, that Beaumarchais gave a dinner party that is generally regarded as the origin of the Société des Auteurs Dramatiques, an organization whose purpose is to defend the interests of playwrights. This was long before the era of copyright law, and Beaumarchais knew from his own

BEAUMARCHAIS

experience how hard it was to protect a play from unwanted changes by the director or, if it was popular, unpaid pirating by rival companies; he also knew how hard it was for the playwright to get paid. At that famous dinner, he got twenty-three dramatic authors to sit down together—which, given the nature of Parisian literary life, must have taken some doing—and to agree to formulate a code of rules and regulations that entrepreneurs would have to obey if they were to be granted permission to produce plays. The Société was, in effect, a playwrights' union, and it still exists today, with a statue of Beaumarchais in the lobby of its office building—which is not, alas, in the Marais.

During his stay on rue Vieille-du-Temple, Beaumarchais also wrote his most influential work, *The Marriage of Figaro*. This sequel to *The Barber of Seville* made explicit the egalitarian viewpoint implied in the original, and if the criticism of the aristocratic lifestyle expressed by the plot weren't enough, there were numerous phrases in praise of liberty not really required by the dramatic action. For this reason the play was rejected by the censors when Beaumarchais first tried to have it performed.

Then the play became a *cause célèbre*, loudly demanded by the public even though very few people had read it. Copies were circulated in England and Russia, where Catherine the Great wanted it staged. Marie Antoinette tried to arrange a private performance at Versailles, but Louis XVI, after reading the script, refused. "We would have to destroy the Bastille if this performance were permitted," was his comment.

Instead the play was performed at Gennevilliers, in a small theater usually reserved for high society amateur productions of light operas for a select audience of friends. Surprisingly, this performance was patronized by the comte d'Artois, one of the two younger brothers of Louis XVI who subsequently became kings of France when the monarchy was restored after the "interlude" of the Revolution and Napoleon. The comte d'Artois (later Charles X) was the head of the most reactionary faction at Versailles; he was also one of its first emigrés, leaving France in July 1789 at the very beginning of the Revolution. He didn't know what he was doing when he permitted Beaumarchais to stage his play with members of the Comédie Française performing.

The scene is described by Mme Vigée-Lebrun: "Beaumarchais was drunk with pleasure; he ran this way and that like a man beside himself; and when the audience began to complain of the heat"—the hall must have been packed—"he didn't take the time to open the windows but instead broke all the panes with his cane, which made people say, after the play, that he had let in fresh air twice."

Public opinion finally prevailed, and on April 27, 1784, the play was staged at the Odéon on the Left Bank, the premier performance in the second theater of the Comédie Française. There was such a crowd trying to buy tickets that three people were crushed to death; because of applause at all the politically pertinent lines the performance took five hours. And just five years later, the Bastille *was* destroyed, proving that for once Louis XVI had been right.

⊚✝◎

RUE DES FRANCS-BOURGEOIS

The street names of medieval Paris (like the gargoyles of Notre Dame) sometimes seem to have been dictated more by fantasy than anything else. There were several *rues des Juifs*, although there were very few Jews; there is a *rue des Mauvais-Garçons* not far away from the corner in the Marais, although what wickedness those lads committed has not made the history books; and what an extraordinary catcher of fish that cat must have been to merit being immortalized by the *rue du Chat-qui-pêche*.

But in the case of rue des Francs-Bourgeois there is a simple explanation. The name does not refer to outspoken proprietors or the unfettered middle class; rather it comes from a charitable foundation, a house of alms that housed forty-eight "bourgeois de Paris" who had fallen on

THE ÉGLISE DES BLANCS-MANTEAUX
"…a fashionable eighteenth-century facade…"

hard times and were therefore exempt from municipal taxes. Today rue des Francs-Bourgeois is the very heart of the Marais, not only for the buildings that line its short length but also for those on the little streets that bisect it from either side. But it is not really very much to look at, especially if you don't take the trouble to go in every entrance door that is open, to step back and look up at a balcony or a decoration, and to wander off on the side streets. In the Marais, as in the rest of Paris, there are some spots that announce themselves as special, worthy of attention, even if at first they are not exactly to your taste. But most of the Marais, much like rue des Francs-Bourgeois, does *not* announce itself at all—it waits to be discovered.

From the house on rue des Rosiers, it is a very short walk up rue Vieille-du-Temple to rue des Francs-Bourgeois. You pass the Hôtel des Ambassadeurs de Hollande and then an informal if trendy little restaurant which is very popular with tourists and residents alike, Le Gamin de Paris. This is right at the corner of rue des Blancs-Manteaux, whose name derives from that of a monastery that was erected on the site in 1258 for an order officially called the "Serfs of the Virgin," a monastic establishment inspired by the example of Saint Francis of Assisi. The monks of this order wore white capes, *blancs manteaux*. Actually the order was dissolved in 1274, after only sixteen years. But the name of the street has survived.

Two other monastic orders subsequently occupied the site: the Guillemites (whose name remains in rue des Guillemites) and then, in the seventeenth century, the Mauristes. It was this last order that built the church of the Blancs-Manteaux that we see from the sidewalk outside Le Gamin de Paris.

The church dates from 1690 and for reasons of space it was built with its entrance facing south and its altar backing up to rue des Francs-Bourgeois. So it is right across the former site of Philippe Auguste's wall. This church, a typical baroque structure, never had a proper facade until 1863. It was then that Haussmann began modernizing the

Ile de la Cité, destroying most of its remaining medieval structures. One of these, the church of the Barnabites, had been given a fashionable eighteenth-century facade in the contemporary neo-Classical style. It is this facade that we see today, transplanted to the front of the seventeenth-century baroque Maurist church.

A short block further up rue Vieille-du-Temple, we arrive at a crossing where three out of four corners are occupied by rather ordinary apartment houses. The reason for this goes back to August 1944, on the day after the Liberation of Paris, when some of the departing German forces lobbed artillery shells into the French capital, an explosive reminder that the war wasn't over yet. A few of these fell at this intersection, destroying almost everything there.

The building on the fourth corner was also heavily damaged by the shells, but it was considered interesting enough to be restored. This is the Hôtel Hérouet, built around 1500 by a Royal Treasurer. The Hôtel Hérouet is a comfortable town house built in a basically Renaissance style, but it is enlivened at the corner by an octagonal little tower with decorations in Flamboyant Gothic, an old-fashioned style for which Parisians retained great affection until the end of the sixteenth century. Putting this fanciful tower on the corner of the town house was probably the equivalent of attaching a Victorian gingerbread porch to a modern beach house. In any event, the house was so thoroughly restored that it all looks Disneyland new. Brigitte Bardot lived there for a while in the sixties.

Walking around to the right side of this town house, we come to a curious little passage or alley leading north from rue des Francs-Bourgeois. The upper stories of the houses to either side project out over the alley; just beyond is one of the entrances to the adjacent Swiss Cultural Center. In some books on the history of Paris this alley is identified as the spot where, in 1407, the band of assassins waited for the Duc d'Orléans before killing him a short block away, where Le Gamin de Paris now offers its fare.

HÔTEL HÉROUET
"...it all looks Disneyland new..."

This bloody event was an episode in a civil war between factions called the Armagnacs and the Burgundians. The King of France at the time was Charles VI, who was intermittently insane. The King and his court resided in the Saint Paul palace, of which no trace remains today, near rue Saint-Paul. The Queen, Isabeau de Bavière, had moved to the Hôtel Barbette, which had been built over a century earlier by a wealthy merchant just a short way up rue Vieille-du-Temple from the gate in the Philippe Auguste wall. The King's brother Louis, Duc d'Orléans, who had taken over affairs of state, paid frequent visits to the Queen at the Hôtel Barbette, visits that set tongues wagging.

It was late in the evening of November 23, 1407, when the king's *valet de chambre* knocked at the door of the Hôtel Barbette with the message that the king wanted to talk to his brother. Ten minutes later Louis appeared, mounted a horse, and set off, preceded by two servants with torches and accompanied by ten armed men. They passed through the gate in the wall, at which point twenty armed men emerged from the darkness. One cut off Louis's hand at his wrist, another split his skull with an axe. Louis's escort fled, as did the assailants. A fallen torch set a pile of straw on fire and the residents of the houses at that corner came running to put it out and prevent the neighborhood from going up in flames. The body of the Duke was carried to the old church of the Blancs-Manteaux, the predecessor of the one standing today.

In reality, given the location of a section of the wall of Philippe August that was still standing at the time, it seems more plausible that the band of assassins waited in the darkness of rue des Rosiers and then attacked when the Duke came through the gate. But what is worth remarking about this small alley is that it still remains one of the few such surviving vestiges of the maze of narrow streets and passageways that connected Medieval and Renaissance Paris. The illusion does not last, for when we continue past the Swiss Cultural Center performing space, we are suddenly at the entrance of the very high-tech showrooms of a lens manufacturing company. And when we turn left, as we are obliged to do, we are in a cobbled courtyard mostly filled with parked cars, with some old-fashioned metal-and-glass repair shops on either side. But if we continue out through a *porte cochère* under an apartment building we find ourselves back on rue Vieille-du-Temple, in front of an elegant eighteenth-century rococo facade. It is this Time Machine aspect, the simultaneous existence of Medieval, Renaissance, eighteenth-, nineteenth-, and twentieth-century structures for residential, commercial, manufacturing, and cultural purposes—all gathered here in one place—that forms one of the intriguing aspects of the Marais.

Rue des Francs-Bourgeois begins at the Place de Vosges. It runs west to rue des Archives, where it changes its name and character, becoming rue Rambuteau. Rue Rambuteau is a neighborhood shopping street for the next two blocks and then, on the other side of rue Renard, where the Marais ends, it becomes one of the jazzy thoroughfares of the recent Beaubourg-les Halles district.

THE ALLÉE DES ARBALÉTRIERS, BY ATGET

When you walk down rue des Francs-Bourgeois you think of it as straight, but it is *not* really straight, as anyone waiting for the east-bound Number 29 bus is acutely aware, since nowhere can you spot an oncoming bus for more than two blocks. But then most of rue des Francs-Bourgeois was probably not a new street at all, even in the thirteenth century; it simply follows an old road that ran along the outside of the Philippe Auguste wall and was turned into a street when the wall came down.

Two blocks after the start of rue des Francs-Bourgeois, you come to rue de Sévigné, named after the Marquise de Sévigné who lived in the Hôtel Carnavalet, the impressive building on the northwest corner. This was her residence for almost twenty years, from 1677 until her death in 1696. Today, Mme de Sévigné is known chiefly for her letters to her daughter, Mme de Grignan, who was fortunately living in the south of France with her husband. When I say "fortunately," I mean it in one sense for Mme de Grignan, who experienced every direct contact with her mother as a catastrophe, and in an entirely different sense for those who have been reading Mme de Sévigné's letters with pleasure for the past three centuries.

It is only in France that volumes of chatty letters filled with the gossip of Versailles and the gossip of Paris, interspersed with effusions of sentiment, could be regarded as one of the masterpieces of National Literature. It is true that these letters contain endless details that delight historical sociologists, but that is not why they are so esteemed. No, they are treasured chiefly for the way Mme de Sévigné uses her words, the way, at times, she seems to create or discover the French language as an instrument for communicating every nuance of feeling, enthusiasm, and judgment while always remaining perfectly grammatical.

This little digression into literature may seem to have led us a long way from the Marais, but no; it is the same qualities that distinguish Mme de Sévigné's prose that distinguish the architecture we see up and down rue des Francs-Bourgeois. One must remember that during most

MADAME DE SÉVIGNÉ

of the seventeenth century, until the Palace at Versailles was completed, the style-setter for all of Europe was still Italy, and more precisely Rome, since this was the era of the great Roman squares and palaces and fountains. The extravagant style of those structures was later derisively called "baroque." At the time the French admired it, but did not particularly want it around at home. Instead they invented an architectural style that delights by its perfect proportions rather than its striking effects. At the beginning of the century—the seventeenth, or "great" century—there was still a good deal of Italianate sculpture and ornamentation on new buildings, although the artists were French. We can see examples of this in the courtyard of the Hôtel Carnavalet and also at the Hôtel Sully, not far away on rue Saint-Antoine. But as time went on French architecture grew more purified and austere, with sculpture and almost all ornamentation banished. You can see this all up and down rue des Francs-Bourgeois—or rather you *can't* see it unless you manage to get inside the *portes cochères,* for this is an architecture that reserves its most imposing facades for the interior courtyard and its

HÔTEL SULLY, GARDEN FACADE

most gracious effects for the hidden garden, turning a deliberately sober face to the street.

The Hôtel Carnavalet is, at present, home to the Museum of the History of Paris, and its extension as far as rue Payenne is nineteenth century, although it incorporates bits and pieces of old architecture from all over Paris. The recently renovated new wing of the museum is housed further up rue de Sévigné in the Hôtel Le Peletier, which was built in 1686 and represents perhaps the height of the French classic style, architecture of a rigor and purity that will not be seen afterward for a century and a half, until the skyscrapers of Mies van der Rohe.

It takes your eye a while to get trained to this style, which may at first simply seem dull. And even when the outer facade is quite handsome, as with the Hôtel d'Albret (at number 31), the very narrowness of the street prevents you from seeing the entire structure. You have to take the time to stand on the opposite sidewalk and turn your head left and right, and then mentally recompose the facade. It is an intellectual exercise, quite appropriate for a highly intellectual style.

Fortunately, that is not always the case. The last house on rue des Francs-Bourgeois is the Hôtel de Soubise. To get there, you walk past the Crédit Municipal, the city pawn shop, a nineteenth-century building whose courtyard contains some remnants of the wall of Philippe Auguste and that also houses a restaurant whose gastronomic quality fluctuates constantly but whose interior, the former domed auction room, is always a delight. And then, across from a café, you find a rather forbidding wall with an imposing archway. You go through the door and then before you is—luxury of luxuries in this crowded district—the *cour d'honneur* with four well-tended lawns, defined to left and right by a horseshoe-shaped colonnade probably inspired by the plaza of Saint Peter's in Rome. The columns are repeated on the ground floor of the facade, and there is a second floor topped by a wide pediment and allegorical sculptures.

The transition from the narrow street to this airy, perfectly ordered

HÔTEL SULLY, COURT FACADE

space is like the opening chord of a symphonic work, and indeed the whole ensemble is the architectural equivalent of a Haydn or Mozart symphony, even if it was built a generation before the Classical style of music was developed. In the past this courtyard was also the entrance to the National Archives; now scholars enter from the rear via rue des Quatre-Fils, passing through a handsome modern building whose lobby offers a view of the garden linking the Hôtel de Soubise and the Hôtel de Rohan, with its thirteen perfectly aligned bays. The Marais always looks backward, but sometimes it also looks ahead.

ΙLE SAINT-LOUIS

The Ile Saint-Louis is not, strictly speaking, part of the Marais, but it is right alongside it and in historical and architectural terms is closely related—at least to the Marais of the great seventeenth-century hous-es. It has its own geographic identity as the island in the Seine just behind the Ile de la Cité, like a large dory trailing an immense yacht, with a splendid rear view of Notre Dame. Baudelaire lived there, as did Daumier. It was on the parapets of its quays that the legendary eigh-teenth century novelist Restif de la Bretonne inscribed the "dates" of his private life, the last of which was still visible in the 1830s. In *Swann's Way*, Proust has Swann living in an apartment on the quai d'Orléans, the bank of the Ile Saint-Louis with the view of Notre Dame. His demi-mondaine lover, Odette, who lives in the fashionable sixteenth arrondissement, cannot understand why Swann, who is otherwise so "chic," would want to live in such an out-of-the-way spot. But the ori-gin of this literary, romantic island is nothing more than the story of a very successful real estate operation.

Before the nineteenth century, Paris relied on firewood, both for heating and cooking fuel. The wood came from forests upstream on the Seine and its affluent the Marne, and was shipped down by water transport. At the eastern end of Paris there was a large port area dedicated to the reception and storage of firewood before it was cut up and distributed throughout the city. Part of this port consisted of two islands: the Ile aux Vaches, upstream, and the Ile Notre-Dame, behind the cathedral. In 1614, two years after the inauguration of what is now the Place des Vosges, a certain M. Marie, who had the post of "general contractor for the bridges of France," had the idea of filling in the space between the two islands to create a new residential area, superbly situated adjacent to the Marais. Marie was joined by two partners in this enterprise, each of whom left his name to a street in the renamed Ile Saint-Louis. Marie himself modestly gave his name to the Pont Marie leading directly to the river front of the Marais, the bridge that was originally the only access to the island.

The street plan was simple: rue Saint-Louis-en-l'Ile, bisecting the island lengthwise, and three cross streets. A modest church was constructed on the central street and consecrated in 1623, but it proved too modest for what quickly became a prestigious neighborhood; twenty years later the original was torn down to be replaced by the baroque structure we see today. Large building lots were sold off and elegant residences constructed, the most elaborate directly facing the quays, with servant's quarters or more modest constructions on the central street. The great building decade was the 1640s, when the Hôtel Lauzun, the Hôtel Lambert, and a dozen others like them were constructed looking out over the Seine. Among those who moved there at that time was Philippe de Champaigne, who left behind the more modest residence of his wife's family on rue des Ecouffes.

While the Ile Saint-Louis may have been built by and for families of wealth and position and has never been home to working-class people, it was never an "exclusive" enclave, the way certain twentieth-century developments are deliberate ghettos for the very rich. Given the structure and habits of seventeenth-century Paris, that was impossible. There had to be a place for servants and shopkeepers and their employ-

QUAI D'ORLÉANS, WITH NOTRE DAME
IN THE BACKGROUND

ees to live. And if the mansions overlooking the Seine, built for the most part by financiers and judges and later often acquired by the nobility, never suffered the comedown and breakup of many mansions in the Marais, they *were* often divided into apartments. So the island became a kind of village in the heart of Paris, isolated and tranquil, surrounded by water and narrow quays, on foggy nights seemingly cut off from the mainland to either side. It appealed to the Romantic temperament. One of its mansions became the Polish Library of Paris, founded in 1838 by Polish exiles and directed by the poet and patriot Adam Mickewicz. The celebrated "club des Hachischins," dedicated to the delectation of the "artificial paradise" produced by cannabis, met in the Hôtel Lauzun, the richly decorated mansion on the Quai d'Anjou that now belongs to the city of Paris and is used for receptions. The poets Théophile Gautier and Charles Baudelaire were sometime participants. Baudelaire had a small apartment on the fourth floor of the Hôtel Lauzun, and even though it looked out on the Seine, it is reported that he had the lower panes of his tall windows frosted so all he could see was sky. The caricaturist, painter, and sculptor Honoré Daumier lived and worked nearby from 1846 to 1863.

The island did not completely escape the ravages of nineteenth-century urbanism, since the Pont de Sully, a prolongation of the Boulevard Henri IV, amputated its eastern end. But as late as the 1950s the island retained its "village" character, with modest shops and cheap restaurants on its central street, although it was already particularly favored by expatriates from many countries, especially Americans. But then tourism and rising real-estate values caught up with it. Today there are no longer any cheap hotels (like the one in which I once lived); they have either been converted into apartments or become fairly expensive. The restaurants are almost all expensive, and a few of them are even worth the tab. The shops are all fashionable.

But the biggest change of all is that Parisians have at last discovered this treasure in the center of their city and made it a favorite Sunday

THE PONT MARIE

afternoon promenade. There is no sense in regretting the past; Paris has always been changing. The pedestrian bridge between the island and the back of Notre Dame is the site every Sunday for musicians and mimes and chalk artists who perform for the milling crowds. There is a pastry shop named Berthillon near the church that makes a specialty of creating superior sherbets. The world did beat a path to its door, and its *sorbets* are now sold everywhere on the island. Despite this, there are still lines of people every Sunday when the weather is good, waiting to buy their cones of fruit ice. In the bad old days *Pravda* once printed a photograph of one of these lines with the caption, "Parisians waiting in line to buy food." Which was perfectly true.

☙❧

THE PLACE DES VOSGES

The Place des Vosges created the Marais in the sense that it was the magnet within whose sphere of attraction many great houses of the Marais were built. It never completely went out of fashion, no matter how dilapidated some of its components might have become at times. And yet, despite the astronomical price per square meter that any apartment commands today, you get the feeling that it has never really been chic! chic! chic! the way the Place Vendôme is chic. There is a middle-class generosity and heaviness to all its proportions, a sacrifice of sleekness to comfort, that betrays its commercial origin, even if that planned commerce never became functional. It is one of the great public spaces of Europe, but one that is no longer used as was intended when it was built. And it has probably never been as beautiful as it is today, with its refurbished public garden and its modest fountains bubbling anachronistically in harmony with the restored facades, whose cheerful ambiance is more historical than elegant.

"Good King Henry the Fourth," as the French often call him, was the prime mover in the creation of the square. As kings go, his architectural ambitions were quite restrained, perhaps because he was the founder of a dynasty rather than an heir of one, a hard-working soldier and an ex-Protestant. The Place Royale—its original name—was planned as a revenue-producing venture, a site for the manufacture of fine textiles, particularly silk. The ground floors were to be given over to shops entered from the generous arcades that provide shelter for the public in bad weather—making this one of the rare pieces of architecture in Paris publicly acknowledging that there ever *is* such a thing as bad weather. The second and third floors were to be factories, with living space in the apartments above. At the same time, a lot of attention and money were spent on giving the square an impressive exterior appearance, in order to make it a fitting stage for those grand processions marking royal arrivals, departures, marriages, and births so beloved in the sixteenth and seventeenth centuries. Paris had previously lacked such a setting; given its purpose, the square was paved with cobblestones and otherwise left completely vacant. It would be the parades, the costumes, the moving stages with their convoluted decors and tableaux, the elaborate fireworks, and the enthusiastic spectators that from time to time would provide furnishings for the space.

The lots were marked out by surveyors and the architectural guidelines clearly established. There would be a "Pavilion du Roi" to span rue de Béarn leading into the square from the north and a "Pavilion de la Reine" spanning rue de Birague to the south—edifices that were never intended for royal residences (despite what tots playing in the modern sandboxes are sometimes told by their nannies), but instead as sites for viewing the ceremonies. With the added prestige of royal sponsorship, sales of the lots were brisk and construction was completed in short order. Perhaps a little too short at times: modern restorations of the arcade vaults have revealed some of them as fakes from the very beginning, plaster ceilings painted to look like brick.

What were never installed, however, were the textile factories that would sell their output in the showrooms below. Instead, the buildings of the Place Royale, considered too good for workshops, were immediately fitted out as residences for the wealthy and titled. Good King Henry was assassinated before the project was complete, and his widow, who was Regent during the childhood of his son, Louis XIII, did not insist on the manufacturing aspect of the venture. Later in the century an equestrian stature of Louis XIII was placed in the center of the square. It remained there for over a hundred fifty years.

During the Revolution, when everything "royal" was anathema, the statue was torn down and the name of the square changed to the Place des Vosges, after the *département* that raised the first volunteer army to repulse the Prussian invasion. But the square itself remained pretty much as it was during all the Napoleonic years when so many other parts of Paris were transformed. Then, fifteen years after the Monarchy was restored, a new statue of Louis XIII was erected where the original had once stood, this time in marble instead of bronze.

THE "NEW" STATUE OF LOUIS XIII

As Paris settled into its long, deliciously slow nineteenth century—slow despite several revolutions and the bloody Commune, delicious with Romanticism, busy as the uncounted middle-class lives that were lived with a Balzacian attention to detail—someone decided to add a bit of green to the former Place Royale, now fallen on hard times. The inspiration was probably a London square, but they put up a very French wrought iron fence with each pole in the form of a pike, and planted some trees and patches of grass. The trees around the statue of Louis XIII, which is still there on its pedestal, were chestnuts, that most Parisian of species. The statue probably towered over them when they were first planted, but eventually the trees grew so tall and dense that they hid the statue, which now cannot be seen from a distance, and always comes as a discovery among the trees.

Over the years many of the original apartments were subdivided, vertically as well as horizontally, with mezzanines and entresols making more by making less of the great original loft volumes. Victor Hugo's apartment at the southeast corner of the square, now a museum, gives a good idea of how the spaces were used at that time, and it is a model of solid middle-class domesticity.

For the first half of the twentieth century the Place des Vosges continued unchanged, simply getting older, of no interest to anyone but historians. But then came the Malraux era, with its declaration that the Marais was an historic district and the fervor for historical authenticity, and the Place des Vosges became one of the most important treasures of the neighborhood. It was immediately proposed not only to clean the facades and restore them to their former glory, but also to return the open space to its original condition: i.e. to remove the fences, pull up the grass, cut down the trees, and pave everything over with large cobblestones. Something similar was being done at the east end of the Louvre, where, under the personal direction of Malraux, a small leafy park was replaced by a moat, revealing the true proportions of the

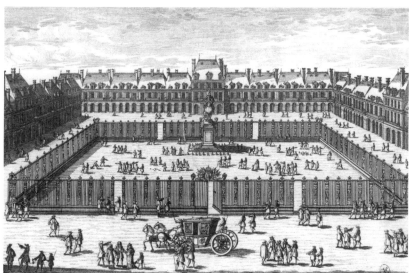

Veüe et perspectiue de la place Royale, a Paris. Le Cardinal Duc de Richelieu y a fait eleuer la St de Louis xiii Roy de France en lan 1639. *fait par Aueline Auec Priuilege du Roy*

THE PLACE ROYALE IN THE EIGHTEENTH CENTURY
"...pave everything over with large cobblestones..."

facade, which includes the colonnade by Perrault, the model for many of the Federal buildings in Washington, DC. That was perhaps a fair exchange in what is, essentially, a business and tourist district. But when the same kind of sterile authenticity was proposed for the Place des Vosges, the only green spot in a densely populated neighborhood, the objections were loud enough to make the authorities abandon the scheme—for the moment, at least.

What happened instead was that for a while the square was neglected. Before, any child who dared profane one of the lawns was systematically chased away by a guard; now, as in Rabelais's Abbaye de Thélème, the policy was, "Do whatever you want!" Inevitably things deteriorated, but when the benches were broken they were not replaced and when the fountains stopped working they were not repaired. And the authorities then proposed a new project, that of constructing a large underground parking garage—which would entail the destruction of the park. But this idea again provoked protests. The inhabitants of the district objected that there were too many cars in the narrow streets of the Marais as it was, and that all the city should do with Place des Vosges was restore the park.

And that, fortunately, is what *was* done, according to the new idea that historical authenticity is not the reconstitution of the appearance of a monument when it was first built, but rather a respect for everything of value that was created during all the years since. Now there are new benches, the grass has been resodded, the fountains spout water most of the time and are even illuminated in the evening. And new rows of lime trees have been planted just inside the newly painted fence.

It is true that the branches obscure the view of the lower half of the red brick and limestone facades, at least during the summer months. But Paris is a northern city and during six months of the year, the leaves of the lime trees, as well as those of the chestnuts surrounding the statue of Louis XIII, are not there. If you want a view of the Place

THE PLACE DES VOSGES
"…on a rare clear day in February…"

des Vosges as it was when it was still the Place Royale, come at noon on a rare clear day in February when the sun, filtered by the bare branches, illuminates the north and west facades of the square. Then you will see the old bricks, as well as the new ones of today's restorations, in the pale light of winter and feel that you are peering through the centuries.

⚜   ⚜   ⚜

My wife, Marianne, would prefer to live in an apartment overlooking the Place des Vosges to any other place on earth, and almost every time we are in Paris she finds a moment to go there. For her the Place des Vosges is her childhood and youth. But we don't live there, which is perhaps just as well. We bought the apartment in the house on rue des Rosiers as a pied-à-terre for our summer visits to Paris when we were living in America, and now that we have moved to France, it is still a pied-à-terre when we go to Paris from our house in the country. It is too cold in the winter and too hot in the summer and too noisy all year round, but surprisingly enough the stairs leading up have not become more difficult; we are used to them. And when I come up from the R.E.R. station at Saint-Michel and find Notre Dame facing me, I still feel something of the same irrational happiness that filled me on my first acquaintance with Paris in the summer of 1949.

"Le Marais"

(EXCERPT)

by Léon-Paul Fargue

THE POET AND WRITER Léon-Paul Fargue (1876-1947) began as a disciple of Stéphane Mallarmé, and his friends included such prominent literary figures as André Gide and Paul Valéry. He is best known today for his tender and fervent evocations of Paris, his native city, and particularly of its older neighborhoods. An avid wanderer, Fargue never hesitated to open a door or look down a byway in order to catch a glimpse of how people lived, and his two works on the capital, *D'après Paris* (1932) and *Le Piéton de Paris* (1939), reflect his fascination with the details of Parisian daily existence.

Like Fargue, I've tried to present a vision of the Marais based on my personal experience, as it was when I first knew it and as it is today, and I offer the following excerpt as a kind of lagniappe, one small echo of the footsteps that have preceded me down these same streets:

It would take volumes and libraries to tell the story of the Marais, so profoundly French is it in every stone, so tied to the wandering of History that human forgetfulness and urban development could do it no harm. Nothing has changed less than the houses of rue des Guillemites, rue de l'Ave-Maria, rue de la Barbette, or rue des Lions. Today as in the past, their former owners could return to their homes without too many surprises. Progress here seems to have arrived in droplets, almost shamefully, for fear of being too modern. The man who bought the Hôtel de Villedeuil, which during the seventeenth century had been occupied by Louis XIV's curious double, the Marquis de Dangeau, once remarked, "The wiring is so bad that it's better simply to use candles."

Just after [World War I], I spent long days acting as guide through the labyrinth of the Marais for a very lovely American woman who had fallen in love with these sumptuous dwellings: the Hôtel Lamoignon, the Hôtel Lefèvre d'Ormesson, the Hôtel de Chalons-Luxembourg with its unforgettable doorway, the Hôtel d'Antonin d'Aubray, the Hôtel de Fleury... In short, she had dreams. And inspired by them she ran to real estate agents and explained in my presence that she absolutely had to buy a house "with ramps, bas-reliefs, spiral staircases, moldings, stone steps, candle snuffers, etc..." Unfortunately most of the houses that had caught her eye were occupied by schools of the City of Paris, pawn shops, museums, bronze casters, bent and near-sighted notaries, associations, government offices, or private individuals who had not the least desire to leave their old lodgings. "But," she said, "I'm going to invite people! I'm going to give receptions worthy of the *Grand Siècle*! of Queen Margot!" Convinced that her charm and money could do anything, even in a city like Paris where public officials are slow and indifferent, she resolved to attack the Marais from on high, and set about inviting ministers, archivists, and ambassadors to her table, in a Palace where even the most official gentlemen always go with pleasure.

One evening, worn out by the supplications of this lady who refused to give up searching for a mansion in the third arrondissement to link her family to "History," a diplomat told her, as seriously as possible, "I've finally found a building that is for sale. It's the most history-filled house you can imagine. The best names of France slept there, loved there, gambled there, killed there—kings, princesses, dukes. The most distinguished, noble, and precious names Paris has to offer are as if by magic linked to this mansion. And what's more, dear friend, I can assist you in purchasing this treasure. We can talk privately in a few minutes in the little salon."

Flushed with excitement, the young American, not realizing the difference between a pearl necklace or fancy car and an old Parisian mansion, declared she was ready to sign a check immediately and move in the very next day.

In a serious voice, the diplomat then told her, "It will cost you two hundred billion..."

Since that day my poor friend has never talked about her desire to live in a sixteenth-century mansion.

The masterpiece of this Marais of a hundred Hôtels, a thousand crisscrossed narrow streets, so dark, so oddly named, so torturous, so hostile to modern traffic that cab drivers always grumble when they go there—the masterpiece of this thoroughly Old Paris—is the Place Royale, now called the Place des Vosges in honor of the first *département* to pay its taxes in the Year VII [under the Revolutionary calendar]. There is profound insight behind this reward: indeed, in these times of difficult budgets, someone should think of giving a medal or a license to sell cigarettes to the first Frenchman every year who fills out his tax return without cheating...

Nothing is less fashionable today than this landscape of bricks wedded to stone, this fanciful architecture that doesn't go with fountain pens, Bugattis, or the light clothing of the High Society of 1939. [...]

In our time, the Place des Vosges is nothing more than the refuge of fortune-tellers, gunsmiths, loan sharks, and modest lawyers. An apartment, a dentist, or a coal seller are all on hand to fit any budget... The Place Royale and the streets of the Marais have been left to the middle-class. The shadows of petty thieves now fall on walls that once received the silhouettes of carriages. Prostitutes with strong shoulders and oiled hair who sit out on the sidewalks with their chairs and their knitting have invaded the charming corners where once young men composed verses when they were not fighting duels, where there was no talk of bicycle races or other sports or elections, but only of love and intrigue.

Is that entire unimaginable, fragile, unique past completely dead? No. Sometimes, from some old house on rue du Pas-de-la-Mule or rue Geoffroy-l'Asnier or rue Barbette, an old, stooped aristocrat emerges, a reminiscence of Capitaine Fracasse, decorated with the Légion d'Honneur and supported by a walker, who looks like he'd gladly expel the Enemy from his neighborhood, where the Kings of France used to visit.

— from *Le Piéton de Paris*

About the Author

ALEX KARMEL was born in Manhattan and educated at Columbia University. His first novel, *Mary Ann* (1958), was made into the film *Something Wild* (1962). This was followed by *Last Words* (1968) and by two books on the French Revolution: *My Revolution* (1970), an historical novel based on the writings of the diarist and "pornographer" Restif de la Bretonne, and *Guillotine in the Wings* (1972). After living for a number of years in Washington, DC, where he wrote theater criticism for the *Washington Review*, Mr. Karmel and his wife moved to France, and now live near Paris.

A Corner in the Marais

was set in a digitalized version of Fournier, a typeface originated by Pierre Simon Fournier *fils* (1712-1768). Coming from a family of typefounders, Fournier was an extraordinarily prolific designer both of typefaces and of typographic ornaments. He was also the author of the celebrated *Manuel typographique* (1764-1766). In addition, he was the first to attempt to work out the point system standardizing type measurement, a system that is still in use internationally. Many aspects of Fournier's personality and period are captured in this typeface, which balances elegance with great legibility. The book was designed by Mark Polizzotti.